T0209728

# BECAUSE I HAVE BEEN THERE

*A Unique Perspective on Parts of the Bible, Based on an Afterlife Experience.*
*Topics that include God, Jesus, Mediumship, Religion, Alien Life, and Disclosure.*

## BOB JACOBS

**BALBOA.**
PRESS

A DIVISION OF HAY HOUSE

Balboa Press books may be ordered through booksellers or by contacting:

Balboa Press
A Division of Hay House
1663 Liberty Drive
Bloomington, IN 47403
www.balboapress.com
1 (877) 407-4847

Because of the dynamic nature of the Internet, any web addresses or links contained in this book may have changed since publication and may no longer be valid. The views expressed in this work are solely those of the author and do not necessarily reflect the views of the publisher, and the publisher hereby disclaims any responsibility for them.

The author of this book does not dispense medical advice or prescribe the use of any technique as a form of treatment for physical, emotional, or medical problems without the advice of a physician, either directly or indirectly. The intent of the author is only to offer information of a general nature to help you in your quest for emotional and spiritual well-being. In the event you use any of the information in this book for yourself, which is your constitutional right, the author and the publisher assume no responsibility for your actions.

Any people depicted in stock imagery provided by Getty Images are models, and such images are being used for illustrative purposes only.
Certain stock imagery © Getty Images.

Scriptures taken from the Holy Bible, New International Version®, NIV®. Copyright © 1973, 1978, 1984, 2011 by Biblica, Inc.™ Used by permission of Zondervan. All rights reserved worldwide. www.zondervan.com The "NIV" and "New International Version" are trademarks registered in the United States Patent and Trademark Office by Biblica, Inc.™

Print information available on the last page.

ISBN: 978-1-9822-3234-4 (sc)
ISBN: 978-1-9822-3236-8 (hc)
ISBN: 978-1-9822-3235-1 (e)

Library of Congress Control Number: 2019910922

Balboa Press rev. date: 08/06/2019

First of all, I want to thank my beautiful, wonderful, loving wife, Barb, who has never doubted or questioned me while on this spiritual journey. Thank you, and I love you!

Secondly, I want to recognize those who have helped me edit my work on this book. Two friends from my spiritual community have revised content structure and edited my draft versions. They have my true thanks for their assistance on this journey.

# In Loving Memory Of

Aiden H. MacMannis

Alexander Massing

Bryn Magree

Chas Bertun

Christina Elizabeth Tournant

Conor F. MacMannis

David Ray Jacobs

Dominique Jasmine Hache

Joshua Thomas Grider

Reece Aaron Andrews

Ross Eric Zimmerman

Our children didn't leave us early, *they simply took a shortcut to grandma's house for dinner.* Upon arrival, they weren't asked to say grace before dinner, they lovingly shared in *God's grace* as they wait for us to return home.

At the onset of writing this book, I was a vengeful, angry, hostile writer, looking to take my wrath out on traditional religion. By the end of writing this book, I realized I am a loving, caring, all-encompassing writer trying to help people who are just like me (Ha Ha). Hey, it is okay to have fun. Spirit loves to have fun. This I know...

# PREFACE

I have always been drawn to the stars. Even as a small child, anytime I went outside at night, it felt like the sky and stars were like a magnetic force pulling on me. From those early days to the present time, I have sensed that there is intelligent alien life in the universe.

So, in 2003, I decided to read the Bible in its entirety. Having always had this sense of alien life, I decided to take notes about anything I read that could possibly be tied to intelligent alien life. I actually wrote the notes in the Bible itself.

Then, in 2014, I had an afterlife experience in which I stood in God's White Light. So now, in addition to years of reading and studying the Bible, I had the real life experience of **knowing** what God was.

The notes I took over 15 years ago went untouched until 2017. That is when I decided to write this second book, which is a continuation of my first book, FIFTY YEARS OF SILENCE NO MORE. My initial idea was to write about what the Bible said about mediumship, but that was about to change. Upon opening my Bible, I studied some of the verses I took notes on all those years ago. That was the defining moment for me. I realized that a lot of the notes I took about possible alien life being described in verses in the Bible, also described a vengeful, angry, jealous, hostile God. Right then it hit me! I knew God wasn't like this. I knew, because I had stood with God.

These notes, that had been lying dormant for over 15 years, told me that the angry God being described in the Old Testament was inaccurate. I believe I took those notes for a reason all those years *ago. I believe it was part of my journey that had already been set into motion. I somehow knew on a soul level that I was supposed to take those notes so that I could explain why and how I know what God is. God is Love.*

*So this entire book is based upon these real life experiences put into motion years ago.*

Having stood in God's White Light in an afterlife experience, I dedicate this book to anyone who is looking to find their peace. May these words help fill your heart with comfort and joy.

"So there is a group of young people in heaven talking with God. God asks them what is troubling them. One of them says that their parents were told by a few members of their church that they didn't go to heaven because they took their own life. God says, 'I don't belong to their church. I AM THE CHURCH.' Another one tells God that his parents were told by a person of a particular belief system that they didn't go to heaven because they overdosed on drugs. God says, 'I don't belong to their belief system. I AM THE SYSTEM.' A third young person tells God that his parents were told that God would be angry with him and take his vengeance out on him for living a less than perfect lifestyle. God replies, 'I am not angry and vengeful. I AM LOVE.' Then another one tells God that his parents were told that he would be cast down for living a life of homosexuality. God replies, 'I do not cast people down for loving one another. I LIFT THEM UP.' Next, collectively, the young people ask God how they could let their families know that they are all right and in HIS SOUL WARMING LOVE AND LIGHT. God tells them not to worry about that because every once in a while He reaches down and touches someone with his Love and Light. He then makes sure that person shares his messages with people like their parents."

Today I am happy to share with you the greatest gift of all. The gift of knowing. I do this…….BECAUSE I HAVE BEEN THERE!

Bob Jacobs

# Contents

# INTRODUCTION

I would like to begin by stating that I was raised as a Christian throughout my life. I attended a Christian church and was baptized as a Christian. So my background is that of traditional religion. Even though I had this traditional religious background, I had to follow my heart and find answers on my own. I wanted these answers to be something that I found in my heart, not something that I had been taught. I had the choice to believe what I had been taught my entire life, or to follow my heart. **I chose to follow my heart.**

My goal while writing this book was to explain what the Bible really does say about God, Jesus, intelligent alien life, and mediumship. I will also touch on the Church and disclosure. Disclosure meaning the government announcing that there is intelligent alien life. This book is a handbook or guide on WHY it doesn't matter HOW you get to God. It will help people (who are just like me) get through and understand how things will ultimately be the same, even after something like disclosure happens. Why I believe that the government hasn't yet came forward and disclosed intelligent alien life will be detailed. The reasons I believe the Church and Religion will still be very important after disclosure will also be explained. Part of this book will be my interpretation of what the Bible also says about the gift of mediumship.

This entire book will be based upon my opinion and interpretation of what the Bible says about all the aforementioned, and other topics. **I will explain throughout this book why it doesn't matter how you get to God.** I will state why even after disclosure happens, the Church, God, and Jesus are still very real and important.

A lot of people might say that they believe in the Bible and live by what it says. I think that is great. Everyone has the right to read and interpret the Bible the way that they see and understand it. That is exactly what I am going to do in this book. I am going to give you my interpretation of what the Bible says about different subjects and topics.

I have always tried to keep an open mind. I have always been drawn to the stars and thought that there must be so much more out there. The universe is so large. How could we human beings be all that there is? I believe in God and Jesus. **I also believe in intelligent alien life.** I am going to explain how different scenarios and different ways of looking at things ultimately lead to the same end result. It doesn't matter how you get there. In my opinion, God and Jesus are both real. It is from my real life experiences and willingness to have an open mind, that I base my conclusions on this *end result*.

I am also a psychic medium. People today call us *mediums*. This means that I talk to people on the other side. By the other side, I am talking about people who have passed from the earth realm. I had an afterlife experience in 2014. This experience awakened my soul and spirit, which led me to develop my mediumship skills. While having this experience, I was fortunate enough to stand in the White Light and presence of God. So I do understand what God is, firsthand.

Since I have stood in the presence of God, I know what it is like in his Light. God is nothing but Love. You have a positive energy running throughout your entire body that culminates in your head. The positive energy pulsates at your head and all you feel is Love. The White Light that you feel is unbelievable. You see the light, but mostly you feel it. The best way that I have heard it described is that it is like taking a bath or swimming in the light. The colors are also very vibrant on the other side. Mostly though, the light and the positive energy of God is what really warms your soul. As you are feeling all of these sensations, you understand telepathically that you are in the presence of, and a part of God. It truly is Spiritual.

When I refer to God throughout this book, I am talking about the God of Love and Light. God is Love. God is the source. I try to use real life experiences to explain things, along with my afterlife education. God in my opinion is not a person. He is a presence. God is everything. Everybody and everything that you see and experience in this world are all a part of God. This *everything* is the *One Consciousness* that we are all a part of.

I have attained a vast amount of afterlife education, which includes reading the entire Bible. My real life experiences of having stood with God, reading the Bible, and attending church service, give me a lot of background in this field. With this background, I am confident that I can speak from experience. **Standing in God's Light gives me insight that most people are not fortunate enough to have.** I have learned from my experiences that God is only about Love. God doesn't care what color your skin is, what religion you practice, or what your politics are. He also doesn't care if you're straight, gay, lesbian, or transgender. God is only about one thing. That one thing is Love!

It is very important as you read this book to understand when I explain what God is and is not, I am telling you from my real life experience of standing in his presence. A lot of topics in this book are not new topics of discussion. But, I believe I offer a very unique perspective. The perspective of having stood in God's light. Please understand that I am also saying that it doesn't matter how you get to God. The end result is the same. As I explain my interpretation of the Bible, I am not saying someone else is wrong and I am right. I am trying to make the point that it is perfectly fine for everyone to take a different path to the same destination. This destination that I am talking about is the eternal Love and Light of God. You may not agree with everything in this book. That is okay. You may not even believe in God. That too is okay. We are all a part of this one consciousness, which I call God.

I try to keep things simple. There is no need to try and make things harder than they need to be. Sometimes you might ask yourself, "Could it really be that plain and simple?" I say yes. So please keep these opening statements in mind as you read this book.

I hope that you can find at least one thing in this book that helps you along in your journey. Even if you don't believe in God, Jesus, or aliens, maybe you can still find that one missing piece of *the puzzle of life* that you are so desperately seeking. Open your mind and your heart will follow. Let your heart find that peace, whatever that may be for you. Always follow your heart.

# PART I

# GOD AND JESUS ARE REAL

# Chapter One

# MY THOUGHTS

Without even knowing it, my research for this book began years ago. That was when I decided to read the Bible in its entirety. The year was 2003. I was 39 years old, and I really wanted to gain insight and knowledge about the history of man on earth. I had gone to church on and off my entire life, but I wanted to really dig in and see what the Bible said for myself. I had also heard people quote the Bible. So I decided that I wanted to find out for myself and reach my own conclusions. I will say that if you read the Bible all the way through, you will more than likely become more spiritual.

For reasons that only now I understand, I took notes on every book in the Bible. At that time, I didn't realize what my purpose was for taking the notes. As I began to put together and write this book, I quickly realized the reason. The notes that I took while reading the Bible were for this book. I do have an open mind. As I went through the Bible, I took notes about all the stories you hear about in Church, Sunday school, and other places. I also took notes about stories that I thought could actually be about intelligent alien life and other topics. That is what this book is all about. In this book I will try to explain how religion, Jesus, churches, alien life, and mediumship, are all a part of God. I will give you my take on what the Bible does say about all of these topics.

I have read dozens and dozens of books on the aforementioned topics, studied online, and attended many webinars. I sit in a mediumship circle. I give mediumship readings, connecting clients to their loved ones on the other side, to people all over the United States. I have my own local mediumship development circle, and I meditate and connect on a daily basis.

But most importantly, I have stood in the presence of God. **I think that alone gives me an edge and a lot of insight.**

My journey has been a life long voyage. I have had paranormal events happen to me my entire life, things like telepathic communication, seeing and hearing spirits, and just a sense of knowing. I kept all of these events that had happened throughout my lifetime a secret. Not even, Barb, my wife of over 28 years, knew about the spiritual side of my life. That all changed when my spiritual awakening occurred in 2014. That is when, Wilma, who is a family friend on the other side of the veil, took me on a journey to the other side, and put me in the presence of God.

More importantly, when you stand in the presence of God, as I did, it changes your life forever. Everything is different after this kind of experience. Ever since the night of my spiritual awakening, I have been like a sponge trying to soak up everything that I could hold. Throughout this book I will share with you what I have discovered. I have been urged forward by my Spirit team (Spirit Guides and Guardian Angels) to assemble this book now. I can feel the urgency.

There is so much negativity in the world today. I think it is time to say, "Hey, slowdown! Listen to your intuition and be a positive force. Walk away from the negativity." I think a good piece of advice today is, "Turn off the electronics and turn on the silence." Take time every day to just sit in the silence somewhere by yourself. You can meditate, pray, listen to nature, or just relax in the silence. This, my friends, is the gateway to finding your inner peace. It is in your heart. Follow it. You have to learn to love yourself first, and then loving everyone else is so much easier.

In Part I of this book, I will finish, using personal experiences, explaining what God is and what God is not. I will also discuss Jesus.

In Part II of this book, I will talk about intelligent alien life and how and where it is described in the Bible.

Part III is about religion and how it has maybe, in some instances, changed the way the Bible is studied and taught. I will also discuss how the Bible is viewed in our culture today.

In Part IV, I will discuss how mediumship (the ability to connect with souls on the other side) is talked about over and over in the Bible. I will also touch on what I believe mediumship is. I will then show how and where the Bible states its case about using mediumship.

After Part IV, I will summarize what I have written and reiterate why I believe it to be true. My primary reason for writing this book was because I wanted to know for myself how all of these topics come together as one. I have amassed many hours researching to compile the contents of this book. The knowledge that I gained, along with my personal experiences, have left me with what I call a twenty-first century approach to God and the Bible. But most importantly, I share this with you **BECAUSE I HAVE BEEN THERE!**

I have found the results of my research to be fascinating. I do want to reiterate right here at the beginning of this book that I am not saying you are wrong if you disagree with me. Rather, I am saying that it is okay to disagree, because in the end it doesn't matter. It really doesn't. It doesn't matter how you get there. The end result is still the same. In my opinion, God and Jesus are both real. My only hope is that you can take at least one thing out of this book to help you along in your journey. Let us get started.

# Chapter Two

# WHAT GOD IS, AND IS NOT

Let me start off by saying that from my personal experience there is only one God. It doesn't matter what religion you are. It really doesn't. Remember, God is the *everything*. We are all a part of this everything. If you walk outside and see a bird singing in a tree, that bird and tree are a part of God. Everything in this world is connected. We are all a part of the same consciousness. I call this consciousness God. **I know this not because of what I have heard or read, but because I have stood with God.** I know it sounds rather odd, but it is true. Wow!

When we pass to the other side, we don't stand in front of a God who is sitting on a throne and wearing a crown. There is no person there as a God waiting to judge us. We judge ourselves. We have a life review. This is done by ourselves or given to us by beings of higher light. These beings can also be known as angels.

God is only about one thing. That one thing is love. God is an all loving presence. He literally is the light. God is the *everything*. God does not sit on a throne and make judgements and demands. Something that I want you as the reader to understand is that I know what God is not, because I have stood in his presence. **I don't pretend to know everything about God, but I can certainly tell you what he is not.**

God does not make demands, such as tithing your income. In my opinion, only a king or ruler would make those demands. Don't misunderstand me here, I believe that God does want us to give generously and help those who are less fortunate than we are. In the Bible, tithing is mentioned in the book of Leviticus.

Leviticus 27:30:"A tithe of everything from the land, whether grain from the soil or fruit from the trees, belongs to the LORD; it is holy to the LORD."

I don't believe tithing is God's command. This is because God is the everything. He wants for nothing. God's love is unconditional, meaning that he doesn't set certain criteria or conditions for us to receive that love. This is a very important point here as you read on through this book. A king or ruler is someone who wants something from other people, not God. Everything already belongs to God. God does want us to give generously. He does not set a standard or demand a certain amount. God does not want what is in your wallet. **He wants what is in your heart.** Anytime throughout this book when I mention God as "he, him, etc.," I am referring to the *God of Love and Light.*

So many times in the Old Testament, God is described as someone who is vengeful, jealous, and a punisher of bad deeds. This is not the God that I have stood with. God is not like this at all. God is said to have killed thousands of people in the Bible. An example of this can be found in the book of Numbers.

Numbers 15:32-36:"While the Israelites were in the desert, a man was found gathering wood on the Sabbath day. Those who found him gathering wood brought him to Moses and Aaron and the whole assembly, and they kept him in custody, because it was not clear what should be done to him. Then the LORD said to Moses, 'The man must die. The whole assembly must stone him outside the camp.' So the assembly took him outside the camp and stoned him to death, as the LORD commanded Moses."

In these verses, the Bible states that Moses was commanded by God to kill the man for working on the Sabbath. Which in turn, he and the people did by stoning him to death. I can tell you straight up, this is not God's will. This is not what God is about at all. I think that this does sound like the will of a king or ruler who was upset that his rules were not followed. This sounds to me like the story of someone who is in charge and is going to make an example out of someone who disobeyed his rules. God is not vengeful like this at all. He is caring and loving. As someone who has stood in the presence of God, I can state beyond the shadow of a doubt, that God would not have anyone stoned to death for working on the Sabbath.

There are also instances in the Bible where God commands the sacrifice of the firstborn son, as an offering. A couple of examples of this are found in the books of Genesis and Exodus.

Genesis 22:2:"Then God said, 'Take your son, your only son, Isaac, whom you love, and go to the region of Moriah. Sacrifice him there as a burnt offering on one of the mountains I will tell you about.'"

Exodus 22:29:"Do not hold back offerings from your granaries or your vats. You must give me the firstborn of your sons."

I can tell you in no way, shape, or form, would God order the sacrifice of children or anybody else. These seem to be orders given by a ruthless ruler. This ruler makes the people follow his rules or suffer the consequences. **So obviously, where I am heading with this is that the people of the Old Testament times were actually, at times, mistaking alien rulers for Gods.** By alien rulers, I am talking about rulers from another solar system, galaxy, or possibly even another dimension. These were the vengeful gods that you so often hear about in the Old Testament.

God is not vengeful.

God is love.

Throughout the Old Testament, the people are warned not to worship false gods. An example of this can be found in the book of Exodus.

Exodus 34:14:"Do not worship any other god, for the LORD, whose name is Jealous, is a jealous God."

In this verse from Exodus, we have a god who is described as being a jealous God. The people are warned not to worship any other gods. Once again, this sounds like a ruler who is trying to gain control over the people so that they don't worship any other ruler. I think the Old Testament, in part, is a documentation of different alien rulers trying to gain control over the people.

I do believe that most of the stories in the Old Testament and Bible are true. I also believe these stories represent events that happened in the chronological manner that they are written. I believe things like the great flood and the birth of Jesus are real events. I also believe that the people of those times had no other way to explain things that made no sense to them at that time. I will get into this in much more detail later in the book. **I know that God is real, but not in the way he is often described in the Old Testament.** As I stated earlier, there is only one God.

In the following verses from the books of Deuteronomy and Jeremiah, there is a loving God who rebukes the sacrifice of people and children. This completely contradicts the other verses in the Old Testament. In these verses, we have a God who is not murderous.

Deuteronomy 12:31:"You must not worship the LORD your God in their way, because in worshiping their gods, they do all kinds of detestable things the LORD hates. They even burn their sons and daughters in the fire as sacrifices to their gods."

Jeremiah 19:4-5:"For they have forsaken me and made this a place of foreign gods; they have burned sacrifices in it to gods that neither they nor their fathers nor the kings of Judah ever knew, and they have filled this place with the blood of the innocent. They have built the high places of Baal to burn their sons in the fire as offerings to Baal- something I did not command or mention, nor did it enter my mind."

In those verses from Deuteronomy and Jeremiah, we have a god being described as a god that disagrees with the policies and rules of other gods. So obviously we have different personalities and different god-like beings, being described as God in the Old Testament. **My point here is that when we talk about the God of the Old Testament, which God are we talking about?** There are clearly several different gods being referenced to in the Old Testament. Think of it in this fashion: if you were a person of that era who had different god-like entities coming from the sky making commandments for you to follow, what else could you think other than that they were gods?

In addition, you could also argue that the verse from Jeremiah could also mean that it isn't the *God of Love* speaking. In this verse he says *nor did it enter my mind*. When he says this, he is making himself sound like a person not God. That is because God is the *everything*. He is the one consciousness and love.

In the book of Joshua, we see where the Lord is said to cherish silver, gold, and other precious metals.

Joshua 6:19:"All the silver and gold and the articles of bronze and iron are sacred to the LORD and must go into his treasury."

God does not care about the peoples' precious metals. God does not keep a treasury of silver and gold.

God is in your heart. **He is not in your bank account.**

God could care less about material things. He does not want you to bring him material things that have no value in the afterlife. When I speak of the afterlife, I am referring to what most people would call heaven. Remember, I have been there!

In the book of Psalms there is a description of many of the vengeful things God did to his people when he was mad at them.

Psalm 78:44-49:"He turned their rivers to blood; they could not drink from their streams. He sent swarms of flies that devoured them, and frogs that devastated them. He gave their crops to the grasshopper, their produce to the locust. He destroyed their vines with hail and their sycamore-figs with sleet. He gave over their cattle to the hail, their livestock to bolts of lightning. He unleashed against them his hot anger, his wrath, indignation and hostility-a band of destroying angels."

Here, God is being said to do a lot of things out of vengeance. He is said to be angry and hostile. In the Old Testament, God is over and over again said to be vengeful, angry, jealous, and hostile.

This is not the God of love that I know on a personal basis.

In the Old Testament, God is sometimes portrayed as a fear based entity.

You have nothing to fear from God. Let me repeat that, **YOU HAVE NOTHING TO FEAR FROM GOD.** He is an all accepting presence of love.

In Part III of this book, I will go into how some religion may have been made into a fear based model in a lot more detail. I want to make the point that God is not fear based in any way, shape, or form.

In the Old Testament, God is portrayed in so many different fashions as a vengeful and angry God. This he is not. **I am not saying that the real God isn't written about in the Old**

11

**Testament.** I am only trying to point out that a lot of times what people thought was God, wasn't. There are many different gods referred to in the Old Testament. Keep these points in mind as we move forward in the next parts of this book.

To summarize this chapter: God is very real. He is a compassionate God who loves everything and everyone. He does not care what your beliefs, religious views, or political views are; nor does he care whether or not you attend services every week. God is not concerned with what color your skin is, or your sexual orientation. He loves everyone. Let me repeat that. He loves everyone. God is everywhere and everything. I hope that this book will help you learn to be a part of this *everything.*

Later in the book, I will talk more about the different gods mentioned in the Old Testament and how they could be different ruling alien beings trying to gain control of the people here on earth. I know this sounds out of the mainstream norm, but open your mind as you read and let your heart decide what to believe. That is very important. Don't let your mind, which has been taught certain things throughout your life, make your decisions. **Let your heart make those decisions for you.** Open your mind and your heart will follow.

So far, I have explained how God is a loving, caring, compassionate God. He does not judge your actions. He is not fear based. He is not jealous, vengeful, murderous, or angry. He is loving.

The question that I have to ask myself at this point is, "Which God of the Old Testament do I want to follow?" My answer, "I choose to follow and stand with the only God. *The God of Love and Light.* The God that I have stood in the presence of." So let us move forward here and finish Part I of this book as we take a look at what I believe Jesus is trying to teach us.

# CHAPTER THREE

# JESUS

**Let me begin by saying that I do believe Jesus is real and a being of higher vibration, divinity, and light.** Jesus is a high level being from the White Light of God. A lot of pictures of Jesus and other religious figures, such as angels, have a halo around their heads. This is a very strong aura that emanates from the head of a being of very high vibration and divinity. These are beings that are very high up in the light on the other side.

Once you get into the New Testament, I think that you start getting a more realistic writing of what happened during those days. The New Testament is full of quotes from Jesus. Mainly in the books of the four gospels; Matthew, Mark, Luke, and John. I noticed while writing this book, that what Jesus talks about in the New Testament does relate to the other side. Having stood in the presence of God, I know what the other side is like. So yes, I do believe that Jesus does talk a lot about the other side, and the details that he uses to describe it I know to be true. There is a difference in following Jesus' teachings and following generations of beliefs passed down by man. I will get into that in a lot more detail in Part III of this book. I will then explain religion in far more detail.

In the New Testament, Mary becomes pregnant with Jesus. Mary's husband, Joseph, is afraid and an angel of the Lord appears to him. The angel tells him that Mary will give birth to a son who is conceived through the Holy Spirit. Joseph is told to call the baby boy, Jesus, because he will save his people from their sins. As Jesus starts to preach, he uses the following theme for his teachings as it says in the book of Matthew.

Matthew 4:17:"From that time on Jesus began to preach, *'Repent, for the kingdom of heaven is near.'"*

I believe when Jesus speaks in this verse, he is speaking of the oneness of God, heaven, and earth. Heaven is all around us at all times. We are surrounded by heaven. I believe that when Jesus said that the kingdom of heaven is near, he was saying that your inner peace and salvation are already within you. They can be found in your heart. We have what is needed to find heaven inside of us right now. It is the essence of forgiveness, peace, love, joy, and connecting with Him. We need look no further than ourselves to find the true salvation and peace that Jesus talks about. As I have stated, *God is the everything.* As a medium, I understand that the other side IS around us all the time.

Also in the book of Matthew, Jesus tells the people that their reward will be in the hereafter. I like to call this *the other side.* He says not to store up material things here on earth because the real treasure is on the other side.

Matthew 6:19-21:"*Do not store up for yourselves treasures on earth, where moth and rust destroy, and where thieves break in and steal. But store up for yourselves treasures in heaven, where moth and rust do not destroy, and where thieves do not break in and steal. For where your treasure is, there your heart will be also.*"

This is a fine example of what I have been saying so far in this book. To find your peace go into your heart, just as Jesus is saying in the book of Matthew. He also talks about rust not destroying your treasure (peace) on the other side, because the peace that Jesus is talking about is eternal. Jesus is also saying in these verses that a thief cannot take your peace away from you. **It is a precious metal (Love) that is in your heart.**

Another bit of advice I have found enormously helpful is learning to live in *the now*. Jesus talks about this in the book of Matthew. This means don't live your life worrying about everything in the world. Live in the present. If you watch most children as they are playing or just being a kid, they are living in the now. Very generally speaking, they don't let the worries of the world ruin their day. I have heard this phrase of *living in the now* put so many different ways; they all are just amazing. In sum, if you can learn to live in the now, you are taking a giant step toward finding your peace. Jesus knew and understood this as he exemplifies so clearly in the following statement.

Matthew 6:34:*"Therefore do not worry about tomorrow, for tomorrow will worry about itself. Each day has enough trouble of its own."*

Jesus really knew exactly what to say. Wouldn't you love to have this guy as your next door neighbor to give you advice? Really that was a trick question. You always have Jesus with you. You can find him in your heart. In this verse from the book of Matthew, Jesus is absolutely telling people to learn to live in the now. It is such an important step in finding the peace that you seek in your heart. This is really starting to get interesting. Don't you think? That was not a trick question this time.

Now let us take Jesus' teachings one step further. Over and over in the New Testament, Jesus is quoted as saying *I tell you the truth*. What does Jesus mean by this? I think Jesus is stating that the truth is your peace, happiness, love, and light. I think Jesus is saying if you can find that truth, then you can find oneness with God. He wants the people to understand how to find their treasure (peace) in heaven. He is telling people to seek the truth and it will guide you in the right direction. **I think that the truth Jesus is talking about is the peace found in being in the *oneness with God*.** I have stood in that truth with God. Jesus wants us to know that the truth will give us that freedom of the eternal light of God, and in some ways, we can actually have it here and now!!

In the book of John, Jesus speaks about being free.

John 8:31-32:"To the Jews who had believed him, Jesus said, *'If you hold to my teaching, you are really my disciples. Then you will know the truth, and the truth will set you free.'*"

Here in these verses from the book of John, Jesus wants the people to know that *the truth will set you free*. This goes along exactly with what I have been speaking about. If you want to live a life of freedom, then find your oneness with God. It truly will set you free. An open heart and mind can lead you to the freedom that can change your life.

What does Jesus say are the real commandments to obey? I think Jesus states ways for people to find their peace in the book of Matthew.

Matthew 22:34-40:"Hearing that Jesus had silenced the Sadducees, the Pharisees got together. One of them, an expert in the law, tested him with this question: 'Teacher, which is the greatest commandment in the Law?' Jesus replied: *"'Love the Lord your God with all your heart and with all your soul and with all your mind.' This is the first and greatest commandment. And the second is like it: 'Love your neighbor as yourself.' All the Law and the Prophets hang on these two commandments."*

**I believe this is where Jesus is saying to open your mind and heart.** Your heart is where you will find your peace and God. The Ten Commandments from the Old Testament are a good way to live and be a good person, but if you are trying to find the peace (truth) that Jesus repeatedly talks about in the New Testament, then this is very important.

The New Testament has many instances where Jesus performs miracles. I believe that Jesus can perform these miracles because he is such an advanced being. Let us take a look at a few such miracles.

Matthew 8:1-4:"When he came down from the mountainside, large crowds followed him. A man with leprosy came and knelt before him and said, 'Lord, if you are willing, you can make me clean.' Jesus reached out his hand and touched the man. *'I am willing,'* he said. *'Be clean!'* Immediately he was cured of his leprosy. Then Jesus said to him, *'See that you don't tell anyone. But go, show yourself to the priest and offer the gift Moses commanded, as a testimony to them.'"*

Matthew 20:29-34:"As Jesus and his disciples were leaving Jericho, a large crowd followed him. Two blind men were sitting by the roadside, and when they heard that Jesus was going by, they shouted, 'Lord, Son of David, have mercy on us!'

The crowd rebuked them and told them to be quiet, but they shouted all the louder, 'Lord, Son of David, have mercy on us!' Jesus stopped and called them. '*What do you want me to do for you?*' he asked. 'Lord,' they answered, 'we want our sight.' Jesus had compassion on them and touched their eyes. Immediately they received their sight and followed him."

Mark 5:24-29:"So Jesus went with him. A large crowd followed and pressed around him. And a woman was there who had been subject to bleeding for twelve years. She had suffered a great deal under the care of many doctors and had spent all she had, yet instead of getting better she grew worse. When she heard about Jesus, she came up behind him in the crowd and touched his cloak, because she thought, 'If I just touch his clothes, I will be healed.' Immediately her bleeding stopped and she felt in her body that she was freed from her suffering."

In these verses, Jesus cures a man who had leprosy, gives sight to two blind men, and a bleeding woman touches his cloak and immediately is healed for the first time in twelve years. These verses from the books of Matthew and Mark, show the strength of the healing light in which Jesus walks. Jesus' soul and body are supreme holders of the White Light of God. This guy was awesome wasn't he? Or I should say, isn't he?

All the topics that I have discussed in this chapter are topics that I can relate to and understand. **Having been to the other side, I can validate that what Jesus teaches us is true.** Also, as a medium, I deal with people on the other side on a daily basis, and they validate that Jesus does speak of what lies on the other side, and what a wonderful treasure it is!

In this chapter I have stated that Jesus is a divine being of very high vibration who performs countless acts of miracles and healing. I have stated that Jesus teaches us that heaven is near (in our heart). Jesus says to live in the now and find the truth. I believe that Jesus is telling us that if we do all these things that he has talked about, then we will find our freedom (our peace). The freedom that I am speaking about is the freedom of having that eternal and internal love and peace in your heart. As I have stated over and over, just like Jesus does in the New Testament, if you want to find your peace then look no further than your heart.

At this point you probably could be asking the following question. If Jesus is the son of God, and you are saying that a lot of the kings or rulers of the Old Testament are potentially alien life forms, then is Jesus the son of an alien life source? Let me answer that by saying, "Does it really matter?" Yes, that is a serious statement/question. Let us say that Jesus was conceived in Mary by an alien ruler from the sky. Also let us say that perhaps many of the gods in the Old Testament were alien rulers or kings, but Jesus came from the real one and only God (the God of love). Either way that you look at it, Jesus was a real being of high divinity and light. **He had supernatural powers that only a divine being could have.**

When it comes to his father it doesn't matter because either way God is the light and essence of everything. God is real. Whether Jesus' father is the one and only God or an alien being from another galaxy, it doesn't matter because God is the everything and Jesus is a divine being. **Either way, Jesus' teachings in the New Testament are the way to the everlasting light.**

In the New Testament, Jesus tells us how to find our eternal treasure. I like to call this *the peace.* If you follow the teachings of Jesus you will find your eternal treasure. Giving your life to Jesus equates to finding your peace. As I stated previously, everything in the universe is a part of God. I speak from experience. **I have stood in the presence of this loving, almighty God.**

To recap Part I of this book, I have explained who and what I believe God and Jesus are. I have also explained how my research for this book started and has continued to now. Keep that mind open.

In Part II, I will explain my thoughts on there being spacecraft mentioned over and over in the Old Testament. So let us now begin Part II of this journey.

# PART II

# ALIEN LIFE IN THE BIBLE?

# Chapter Four

# LET'S NOT OVER THINK THINGS

Let us start this chapter by putting ourselves in the position of the people on planet Earth two thousand or more years ago in the days of the Old Testament. Let us say that in those days you were out in the wilderness alone with your family at night and a helicopter happened to start hovering above where you stood. Taking this scenario further, let us say that as it hovered in place above you, someone inside the helicopter shined a spotlight down upon you. As the blinding light came down from the night sky into your eyes, someone in the helicopter started speaking over a very loud external speaker. At the same time, different colored lights flashed inside and outside the helicopter. As the voice from the helicopter started speaking, this is what it said, "I am here to help you and save you. Listen to what I have to say. It is very important. Take your family North to the caves in the hillside. You will be safe there. Do not hesitate, go now."

So let us say that you heeded the warning of this entity from the sky. As soon as you entered the safety of the caves, a terrible storm full of lightning bolts ravaged the entire area. The only safe place was the caves that you and your family were in. What would you tell your friends happened that night? Would you even tell them? How would you describe what you saw and heard? This entity just saved you and your family's lives. How could it know there was a storm coming?

I think the conversation would go something like this; "Friends, God came from the night sky above. His presence made a roaring sound. His light shined very brightly. His appearance was very colorful. His voice was thunderous. He left in the sky as quickly as he entered in the sky. It had to be God. How else would he know about the storm coming? Only God could do this. He saved me and my family's lives. I am forever grateful and owe him my gratitude for eternity." I think this statement would be pretty close to what a person would say in that time period and situation. How else could you describe it?

Now let us imagine if it wasn't a helicopter, but some type of spacecraft. I really do not think it would matter which one it was, because both the helicopter and the spacecraft would have the same effect on the people of those days. Just the other day, my wife and I were at an outdoor amphitheater with some family members listening to live music. As the sun set, a drone started flying above us taking video of the city. The drone had two red lights on it. I realized that if only fifty years ago I had seen that drone up close, the two red lights would have looked like red eyes to me. How else could I have explained that just fifty short years ago?

So my point obviously is: Look at the difference between fifty short years ago and two thousand years ago. I can only imagine what would have gone through people's minds two thousand years ago if they saw something like a drone, helicopter, or some other flying object; especially if it was speaking directly to them and they saw it at night. Clearly people living in the those times being up close and personal with any type of motorized flying machine, would have a hard time understanding what they saw. They would also have a hard time describing it. They would have to, in one way or another, consider the flying entity a God-like entity.

Next let us touch briefly on ancient structures that are spread out around the world. There are pyramids, rock formations, earth mounds, and astrologically lined up structures that monitor the solstices. There are also cave carvings and drawings, ancient texts, etc. These artifacts are thousands of years old. A lot of scientists of today still aren't sure or do not agree upon how some of these structures were built. The technology was primitive back in that time period.

The pyramids of Egypt are an amazing feat even if you built them today. The large stones used on these pyramids were cut precisely and accurately. Let's first just think about how they moved the very large boulder-like stones and got them to the height that they needed them. **This alone would be a monumental task even with today's technology.** Secondly, with the tools people had thousands of years ago, how did they make such perfect and precise cuts on the large stones that they moved? Also, consider the fact that ancient pyramids are on several different continents, with many of them being built very similarly. It would be different if these ancient artifacts were single instances, but they are not. They are found around the globe.

How can we explain these different types of structures being built by very ancient and primitive cultures? I think the answer is very simple. Things are what they are. Don't try to overthink things. Keep it simple. Is it necessary to make everything in history, and on our planet, fit our model of thinking? Why make it hard? I believe that a lot of ancient structures found around the globe were built with the help, and design, of alien beings. It is what it is.

I realize that when I start talking about intelligent alien life, I lose some people. That is okay. That is the whole point of this book. It doesn't matter how you get there. God and Jesus are both real. A lot of people have been taught certain applications about God their entire lives. I am one of those people. Just because something wasn't what we were brought up to believe or not what we were taught, doesn't mean that it isn't true. A lot of people live by the Bible and say that if it isn't in the Bible then it isn't true. Fair enough, but I contend that the Bible does speak a lot about alien life; mainly in the Old Testament. It is up to us to interpret the Bible. *It doesn't matter who is right.*

The universe is so vast and immense. Our Milky Way galaxy alone has billions of stars. With an open mind, consider how the possibilities are limitless when it comes to the number of stars and potential alien life. I believe the number of intelligent life sustaining planets in our galaxy alone would be staggering or mind blowing to a lot of people. Remember, you must try to keep an open mind. The universe allows for it. So why not be a part of it? Instead of fighting the natural forces of the universe, flow with it. God IS the universe. Be a part of God. He will not lead you astray. God is good, even to other alien life forms. They are a part of the same God as we are.

Always remember as we move forward, that what I believe goes against a lot of what I was taught and believed my entire life. **I say again, IT DOESN'T MATTER HOW YOU GET THERE. GOD AND JESUS ARE BOTH REAL.** In subsequent chapters, I will go into further depth on this subject of alien life as it pertains to the Old Testament.

I know that it seems like I am getting a little off track here, but I am letting some very important information sink into your mind before the next chapter. I am setting the stage for the next chapter where I will point out in more detail what I believe the Bible says. My point thus far in this chapter is this; Let us not overthink things in life. Let us take things as they are. The helicopter scenario in this chapter will help you understand how I arrived at my conclusions in the next chapter. I have mentioned the difficulty of engineering, drawing, and building, ancient artifacts with the technology of those days.

I realize it can be difficult to accept some of my ideas. They certainly are different from what I was taught my entire life. But let us open our minds to the simplicity of things.

I choose to go with the universe, not against it.

God is the universe.

Everything in the universe is a part of God.

However you look at things, remember that everything in the universe is interconnected and a part of God.

**WE ARE ALL A PART OF THE ONE CONSCIOUSNESS.**

**I call this one consciousness God.**

# CHAPTER FIVE

# DOES THE BIBLE HAVE DOCUMENTATION OF SPACECRAFT?

I contend and believe that the Bible has many instances where spacecraft are being described. The Old Testament has an abundance of these stories. I will point out many of them. So yes, since I believe there were spacecraft being described in the Old Testament, then I do believe there were alien beings guiding and piloting these spacecraft. I found these verses in the Bible over fifteen years ago, as I read and took my notes. I had no idea at the time that these notes would be used to help write this book.

My belief is that, in the Old Testament, there were alien kings and rulers fighting for control over the people. Many of these spacecraft that the aliens flew were thought to be God-like to the people of that time. How else could they present and describe what they saw and heard in these verses? They were a people living in a primitive culture. But let me make it clear that I do believe in God and Jesus. **I am not trying to disprove the existence of God.** I am trying to point out that the Old Testament may have been partly misinterpreted over the years.

Keep an open mind as you read through the following Bible verses. Try to put yourself in the shoes of the people of those days. Think about how they would describe what they saw and heard. If you take the Old Testament for what it is and says, instead of trying to make the verses fit a certain set of beliefs, then you may also come to some of the same conclusions as I have.

In the book of Exodus, Moses hears God speaking from within a burning bush. Moses also comes down from Mt. Sinai after meeting with God. When he returns, his face is radiant red.

Exodus 3:1-6:"Now Moses was tending the flock of Jethro his father-in-law, the priest of Midian, and he led the flock to the far side of the desert and came to Horeb, the mountain of God. There the angel of the LORD appeared to him in flames of fire from within a bush. Moses saw that though the bush was on fire it did not burn up. So Moses thought, 'I will go over and see this strange sight-why the bush does not burn up.' When the LORD saw that he had gone over to look, God called to him from within the bush, 'Moses! Moses!' And Moses said, 'Here I am.' 'Do not come any closer,' God said. 'Take off your sandals, for the place where you are standing is holy ground.' Then he said, 'I am the God of your father, the God of Abraham, the God of Isaac and the God of Jacob.' At this, Moses hid his face, because he was afraid to look at God."

Exodus 34:29:"When Moses came down from Mount Sinai with the two tablets of the Testimony in his hands, he was not aware that his face was radiant because he had spoken with the LORD."

In Exodus 3, when Moses was spoken to by God from within a burning bush, he began to walk toward the bush. He then heard God's voice from within the bush say, *do not come any closer.* This seems like an entity telling Moses not to come any closer, because the fire from the engines or propulsion system of a craft could hurt him. Also these verses say that Moses hid his face because he was afraid to look at God. This may be one of the most important lines in this book. I can tell you from experience that when you are in the presence of God, you have absolutely no fear. You feel only love. Let me repeat that: **When you are in the presence of God, you have absolutely no fear.** Only the feelings of love.

In Exodus 34, Moses came down from Mount Sinai with a radiant red face. It seems pretty clear to me that Moses may have been burned by the radiation from a propulsion system. I try to take things as they are, not what they are supposed to be by a set belief. I realize it might seem as if these two sets of Bible verses that we start this chapter with seem insignificant. In reality, they are of the utmost importance to get us started in the right direction. I know from experience that God's light does not burn your skin. I have stood in that light. It does not burn your skin. **It warms your soul.**

In the book of Leviticus, God is associated with fire, as he so often is throughout the Old Testament.

Leviticus 10:2: "So fire came out from the presence of the LORD and consumed them, and they died before the LORD."

God does not have a presence of fire. God has a presence of soul warming light. Could this again be fire from some type of propulsion system or even a weapon of some type?

31

In the book of Numbers, Moses leads the Israelites through the wilderness. In doing so, they follow a cloud.

Numbers 9:15-22:"On the day the tabernacle, the Tent of the Testimony, was set up, the cloud covered it. From evening till morning the cloud above the tabernacle looked like fire. That is how it continued to be; the cloud covered it, and at night it looked like fire. Whenever the cloud lifted from above the Tent, the Israelites set out; wherever the cloud settled, the Israelites encamped. At the LORD'S command the Israelites set out, and at his command they encamped. As long as the cloud stayed over the tabernacle, they remained in camp. When the cloud remained over the tabernacle a long time, the Israelites obeyed the LORD'S order and did not set out. Sometimes the cloud was over the tabernacle only a few days; at the LORD'S command they would encamp, and then at his command they would set out. Sometimes the cloud stayed only from evening till morning, and when it lifted in the morning, they set out. Whether by day or by night, whenever the cloud lifted, they set out. Whether the cloud stayed over the tabernacle for two days or a month or a year, the Israelites would remain in camp and not set out; but when it lifted, they would set out."

These verses speak of a large cloud that the people followed. By day it looked like a cloud. At night it looked like fire. Verses like these need to be interpreted as they are described. I see some type of flying object with a propulsion system being described. Or possibly, and simply, lights. **In those days, how else would they describe something of that nature?**

The book of Deuteronomy says God gave Moses the two stone tablets with the Ten Commandments. He was said to be coming from within a fire.

Deuteronomy 5:22-27:"These are the commandments the LORD proclaimed in a loud voice to your whole assembly there on the mountain from out of the fire, the cloud and the deep darkness; and he added nothing more. Then he wrote them on two stone tablets and gave them to me. When you heard the voice out of the darkness, while the mountain was ablaze with fire, all the leading men of your tribes and your elders came to me. And you said, 'The LORD our God has shown us his glory and his majesty, and we have heard his voice from the fire. Today we have seen that a man can live even if God speaks with him. But now, why should we die? This great fire will consume us, and we will die if we hear the voice of the LORD our God any longer. For what mortal man has ever heard the voice of the living God speaking out of fire, as we have, and survived? Go near and listen to all that the LORD our God says. Then tell us whatever the LORD our God tells you. We will listen and obey.'"

In these verses, Moses receives the Ten Commandments from God. God is said to be in a cloud of fire. I believe these verses resonate very strongly with the helicopter scenario that I stated at the beginning of chapter four. Another point that I want to make here is the people say they will *listen and obey* God. This also reminds me of the helicopter story. In this story, the man took his family to shelter. He listened to and obeyed the voice from the helicopter. If a voice came from an object in the sky in the times of the Old Testament, wouldn't you listen to and obey it too? I see a lot of similarities and parallel lines between these two stories. So many times in the Old Testament God is associated with fire. God does not associate with fire as his light. **His light is the light of love and peace.**

Also found in the book of Deuteronomy, is the story of Moses leading his people across the Jordan River.

Deuteronomy 9:2-3:"The people are strong and tall-Anakites! You know about them and have heard it said: 'Who can stand up against the Anakites?' But be assured today that the LORD your God is the one who goes across ahead of you like a devouring fire. He will destroy them; he will subdue them before you. And you will drive them out and annihilate them quickly, as the LORD has promised you."

Here, the Bible speaks of God destroying people like a devouring fire. It also speaks of God going ahead of the people and clearing the way for them like a devouring fire. I believe the Bible is speaking of some type of craft that would go ahead of the people, and do what is necessary to clear the way for them. It says that God will destroy them. **God does not destroy people.** I do think that this sounds very much like a military move, of modern times, using aircraft with fire power.

Also in the book of Deuteronomy, God tells Moses what he is going to do to his people after they turn to other gods.

Deuteronomy 31:15-18:"Then the LORD appeared at the Tent in a pillar of cloud, and the cloud stood over the entrance to the Tent. And the LORD said to Moses: 'You are going to rest with your fathers, and these people will soon prostitute themselves to the foreign gods of the land they are entering. They will forsake me and break the covenant I made with them. On that day I will become angry with them and forsake them; I will hide my face from them, and they will be destroyed. Many disasters and difficulties will come upon them, and on that day they will ask, 'Have not these disasters come upon us because our God is not with us?' And I will certainly hide my face on that day because of all their wickedness in turning to other gods.'"

In these verses we hear about God in a pillar of a cloud. This sounds like a possible spacecraft to me. God tells Moses that his people will worship other gods. God knows that there are no other gods. He does not have to compete with other gods. He knows this. God does not go around worrying about people obeying other gods. I believe this sounds more like a king or ruler, not God. God tells Moses that he will become angry with them. He says that he will turn his back on them and let them be destroyed. God does not get angry. He certainly would not turn his back on them. Every single soul out there is a part of God.

This is a perfect example in the Old Testament of a jealous and vengeful God. This God is willing to kill, conquer and destroy. God also speaks of foreign gods in these verses. The whole story sounds very much like military leaders fighting for people and land. Could this be the story of a conflict between different alien leaders? They would certainly be considered God-like to people of that time period. Doesn't this sound like different alien leaders fighting for control over the land and the people of the earth? These verses could be taught by some as being a fear based belief. If you follow Jesus' words in the New Testament, he will lead you to God (The Peace). You have absolutely nothing to fear from God.

In the book of 1 Samuel, we have a story about the Ark of the Covenant.

1 Samuel 5:10-11:"So they sent the ark of God to Ekron. As the ark of God was entering Ekron, the people of Ekron cried out, 'They have brought the ark of the god of Israel around to us to kill us and our people.' So they called together all the rulers of the Philistines and said, 'Send the ark of the god of Israel away; let it go back to its own place, or it will kill us and our people.' For death had filled the city with panic; God's hand was very heavy upon it."

These verses mention, *the god of Israel*. There are not different gods for different regions on earth. There is only one God. In these verses the people are afraid of the Ark of the Covenant. Wherever it had been, people had died. Some also had tumors develop on their bodies. Could the ark be a technologically advanced device that puts off radiation? People dying and having lesions and tumors on their bodies when they are around the Ark of the Covenant sounds a lot like people being poisoned by radiation or some other type of weapon. I try to take things as they are, not what my culture has taught me.

Also in the book of 1 Samuel, there is the story of David and Goliath.

1 Samuel 17:4:"A champion named Goliath, who was from Gath, came out of the Philistine camp. He was over nine feet tall."

I believe in this verse Goliath could be a being from an alien race. He was almost twice as tall as other humans.

In the book of 2 Kings, there is the story about the prophet Elijah.

2 Kings 2:11:"As they were walking along and talking together, suddenly a chariot of fire and horses of fire appeared and separated the two of them, and Elijah went up to heaven in a whirlwind."

This verse is the story of Elisha and Elijah walking. It speaks of a chariot of fire from the sky which takes Elijah up to heaven in a whirlwind. First of all it says *chariot of fire*. It doesn't say God. **So let us be clear here, the Bible speaks of a *chariot of fire* in the sky.** I believe that only leaves the explanation of it being a flying craft of some kind. The fire it mentions would have something to do with the propulsion system of the flying craft. The whirlwind that the Bible speaks of, taking Elijah up to heaven, would most definitely be a description of something happening as Elijah is taken to heaven (the sky). I believe this could be a whirlwind of dust being caused by the ship as it hovered. It could also be some kind of light beam causing confusion to Elisha as he watched. Or could it be some kind of advanced tracking beam used to transport people?

I would like to make the point that in the Old Testament, people like to refer to heaven as being in the sky. We still do this today. I believe this originated from people calling the spacecraft they saw, *God*. I do believe that heaven (the other side, as I like to call it) is in the sky because it is all around us. Remember, I know from my experience of standing with God that He is everywhere and everything.

In the book of Job, God speaks from within a storm.

Job 40:6:"Then the LORD spoke to Job out of the storm:"

Over and over again, God is said to be associated with storms or things associated with the sky. Is this another example of how some fear based beliefs have been passed down from generation to generation over long periods of time? I can't stress enough how monumental the following example shows how some young children are taught that they need to fear God.

Just the other day, I was outside at a public event with my family when it started to thunder and lightning. As it started to thunder and lightning, I heard a young girl ask if the thunder and lightning meant that God was mad. I think this is a perfect example of the point that I am trying to get across. I realize this was an innocent statement from a young child that had no agenda contained in it. But, what she said is monumental in confirming that the Old Testament can be taught as a fear based way of trying to keep everybody on the straight and narrow. If we pay attention and listen, the very young children of the world can teach us so much.

Just think if we taught our children that God is only Love. Most of the time God is taught as love, but he can also be presented as someone who will get angry and get revenge if you are not good. Some children are taught to fear God at a very young age. If a child is being taught that it is okay for God to be angry, jealous, vengeful, and murderous; just think what that is telling them they can be. They certainly would have to think that if it is okay for God to be like this, then it is okay for them to be like this. I believe some people may live a life of fear based beliefs because they were taught fear starting at a very early age. God is not like this. God is only Love.

In the book of Psalms, David the shepherd boy gives a description of God.

Psalm 18:7-13:"The earth trembled and quaked, and the foundations of the mountains shook; they trembled because he was angry. Smoke rose from his nostrils; consuming fire came from his mouth, burning coals blazed out of it. He parted the heavens and came down; dark clouds were under his feet. He mounted the cherubim and flew; he soared on the wings of the wind. He made darkness his covering, his canopy around him- the dark rain clouds of the sky. Out of the brightness of his presence clouds advanced, with hailstones and bolts of lightning. The LORD thundered from heaven; the voice of the Most High resounded."

I sit here in awe as I read the verses above. My notes from over fifteen years ago, point out a part of the Bible that goes hand in hand with the helicopter scenario that I spoke about at the beginning of chapter four. Take a moment and flip back to the first page of chapter four. Look at the similarities of the helicopter story and this story told by David the shepherd boy. Look at the similarities of what I am trying to point out in this story from the book of Psalms.

The next two verses are also from the book of Psalms. God is being described as a personality. His appearance is also being described as he arrives.

Psalm 21:9:"At the time of your appearing you will make them like a fiery furnace. In his wrath the LORD will swallow them up, and his fire will consume them."

Psalm 68:4:"Sing to God, sing praise to his name, extol him who rides on the clouds- his name is the LORD- and rejoice before him."

These are again examples of how God is described as a God of wrath and fire. He also is said to enter on the clouds. I know by now you are probably getting a little tired of my repeating this, but God is not wrathful and he is not associated with fire. I also have to again mention how God is, most of the time, making his appearance from the sky.

*Having stood in the presence of God, I can tell you that we are surrounded by God at all times. He is not just in the sky. He is everywhere. God is all that is.*

Also in the book of Psalms, God is being described as Moses leads his people through the wilderness.

Psalm 78:14:"He guided them with the cloud by day and with light from the fire all night."

This to me sounds like a description of a spacecraft that Moses and his people are following. During daylight it looks like a cloud. At night the craft could have turned on some type of light to guide the people. Also the propulsion system would likely be more visible at night.

Next in the book of Psalms, we have the story of Moses and his people being fed by God as they moved ahead in their journey through the wilderness.

Psalm 78:24-25:"he rained down manna for the people to eat, he gave them the grain of heaven. Men ate the bread of angels; he sent them all the food they could eat."

These verses seem like nothing more than an air drop. In today's modern world we have air drops like these all the time.

Our military, among other agencies, drops food from the sky all the time. This could be for people in war-torn countries or people surviving natural disasters. **I will not try to overthink these verses and make them fit some model of existence that I have been taught.** I believe the answer is very simple. The beings inside the spacecraft are feeding Moses and his people. They do this so that they may continue towards the land that these beings want them in.

Next up in the book of Psalms, David describes how he understands what God is.

Psalm 78:49:"He unleashed against them his hot anger, his wrath, indignation and hostility- a band of destroying angels."

Here again, God is being described as everything that he is not. God is not angry, wrathful, or hostile. God is not like this. It sounds more like the description of a war-like captain of a spacecraft, doesn't it? Regarding the *band of destroying angels*, doesn't that sound a lot like small spacecraft leaving a mother ship to wreak havoc?

I want to mention one other verse from the book of Psalms.

Psalm 104:3: "and lays the beams of his upper chambers on their waters. He makes the clouds his chariot and rides on the wings of the wind."

I believe the verse above is simply nothing more than a person of the Old Testament days describing something that was not describable to them. If someone arrived in the sky in those days, the flying machine would have to be thought of as God-like.

I want to list a few more verses. This time from the book of Isaiah. These verses also describe God as angry, wrathful, and associated with fire. One of the verses also says that God rides on a swift cloud.

Isaiah 19:1:"See, the LORD rides on a swift cloud and is coming to Egypt. The idols of Egypt tremble before him, and the hearts of the Egyptians melt within them."

Isaiah 30:27-28:"See, the Name of the LORD comes from afar, with burning anger and dense clouds of smoke; his lips are full of wrath, and his tongue is a consuming fire. His breath is like a rushing torrent, rising up to the neck. He shakes the nations in the sieve of destruction; he places in the jaws of the peoples a bit that leads them astray."

Isaiah 30:33:"Topheth has long been prepared; it has been made ready for the king. Its fire pit has been made deep and wide, with an abundance of fire and wood; the breath of the LORD, like a stream of burning sulfur, sets it ablaze."

When God is said to ride on a swift cloud, I believe the adjective *swift* may be referring to the speed, maneuvering ability, and other attributes of a flying ship. I believe the cloud being mentioned is in reference to a spacecraft. These verses refer to smoke, fire, and shaking. This sounds like nothing more than a description of a flying machine.

If you went outside today, and a jet plane roared past you at a very low altitude, you might see fire from the jet engine. You might even see dust being blown up in the air as it passed. You could possibly feel a vibration around you as the jet passed by. Let us say that you stood outside with a person of the Old Testament days and this same jet airplane flew past. After its passing, you were both taken to separate rooms and were told to give a description of what you saw. I can only imagine what the differences in the description of the jet airplane would be.

In this final story in the book of Isaiah, there is also mention of God coming with his chariots. In these verses, *chariots* is used and meant to be recognized in a plural fashion.

Isaiah 66:15-16:"See, the LORD is coming with fire, and his chariots are like a whirlwind; he will bring down his anger with fury, and his rebuke with flames of fire. For with fire and with his sword the LORD will execute judgement upon all men, and many will be those slain by the LORD."

First of all, as it does so many times in the Old Testament, the Bible speaks of God killing people with fire. As I have said over and over, God is not like this. In these two verses the word *chariot* is used in a plural fashion. This verse sounds a lot like a description of a squadron of spacecraft. These craft were using some type of weapon that people of that day would describe as fire. This story sounds like nothing more than a description of a squadron of flying machines launching an attack on a very primitive culture of people. So again, to them this would have to be God doing this to them.

Next, I want to touch on one verse from the book of Jeremiah.

Jeremiah 4:13:"Look! He advances like the clouds, his chariots come like a whirlwind, his horses are swifter than eagles. Woe to us! We are ruined!"

This sounds like people who know that they are outgunned by a force that is far greater than them. This verse talks about how graceful the chariots are. Again the word chariot is used in a plural fashion. Most of us have been to some type of air show. We have seen how swift and graceful a squadron of planes can be as they fly in unison. Imagine someone of the Old Testament days standing next to you at an air show. Can you imagine what their reaction would be compared to yours?

Next we will move forward to the book of Ezekiel. I am quoting around twenty verses in here from this book. The utter importance and sheer magnitude of these verses describe what would seem to be a spacecraft of some type. In the entire Old Testament, I believe these verses and many other verses from the book of Ezekiel have the best descriptions of spacecraft. **If you are looking for a connection in the Bible and intelligent alien life, then you need to look no further. This is it.**

Ezekiel 1:4-24:"I looked, and I saw a windstorm coming out of the north- an immense cloud with flashing lightning and surrounded by brilliant light. The center of the fire looked like glowing metal, and in the fire was what looked like four living creatures. In appearance their form was that of a man, but each of them had four faces and four wings. Their legs were straight; their feet were like those of a calf and gleamed like burnished bronze. Under their wings on their four sides they had the hands of a man. All four of them had faces and wings, and their wings touched one another. Each one went straight ahead; they did not turn as they moved. Their faces looked like this: Each of the four had the face of a man, and on the right side each had the face of a lion, and on the left the face of an ox; each also had the face of an eagle. Such were their faces. Their wings were spread out upward; each had two wings, one touching the wing of another creature on either side, and two wings covering its body. Each one went straight ahead. Wherever the spirit would go, they would go, without turning as they went. The appearance of the living creatures was like burning coals of fire or like torches. Fire moved back and forth among the creatures; it was bright, and lightning flashed out of it. The creatures sped back and forth like flashes of lightning. As I looked at the living creatures, I saw a wheel on the ground beside each creature with its four faces. This was the appearance and structure of the wheels: They sparkled like chrysolite, and all four looked alike. Each appeared to be made like a wheel intersecting a wheel. As they moved, they would go in any one of the four directions the creatures faced; the wheels did not turn about as the creatures went. Their rims were high and awesome, and all four rims were full of eyes all around. When the living creatures moved, the wheels beside them moved; and when the living creatures rose from the ground, the wheels also rose. Wherever the spirit would go, they would go, and the wheels would rise along with them, because the spirit of the living creatures was in the wheels. When the creatures moved, they also moved; when the creatures stood still, they also stood still; and when the creatures rose from the ground, the wheels rose along with them, because the spirit of the living creatures was in the wheels. Spread out above the heads of the living creatures was what looked like an expanse, sparkling like ice, and awesome. Under the expanse their wings were stretched out one toward the other, and each had two wings covering its body. When the creatures moved, I heard the sound of their wings, like the roar of rushing waters, like the voice of the Almighty, like the tumult of an army. When they stood still, they lowered their wings."

All I can say is wow! Are you kidding me? I have read this over and over. The more I read it, the more I understand that Ezekiel's description about his encounter with God is nothing more than a description of some type of flying machine. I find it very interesting that in all of those verses, I don't see the word God. I do see the words *man* and *creature*.

Let us imagine ourselves standing outside with a person of those days. Now imagine this object being described by Ezekiel coming into our view. I believe the Old Testament person would describe something very similar to what Ezekiel described. On the contrary, our description would simply be something like, "Dude, you should have seen this UFO that I saw last night. It was something right out of a sci-fi movie."

I am going to list a few key words or phrases out of these verses. Next to them, I am placing what I think these key words could be or mean. You will have to judge for yourself. I won't take these verses and make them fit what I have been taught my entire life, rather I take these verses *simply* as they are written.

FLASHING LIGHTS/ LIGHTNING- Aircraft lights or strobes.

GLOWING METAL- Structural parts of the ship.

FIRE- A propulsion or engine system, or the exhaust from said system.

LIVING CREATURES- Moving parts and/or alien beings.

LEGS- Landing gear.

FEET- Landing gear.

BURNISHED BRONZE- Structural parts of the ship.

WINGS THAT TOUCH EACH OTHER- These could possibly be rotors like a helicopter has, set abreast, next to each other.

TORCHES- Lights or propulsion/engine system.

FLASHES OF LIGHTNING- Strobes or aircraft lights.

WHEELS ON THE GROUND- Wheels.

CHRYSOLITE- Different colors.

WHEEL INTERSECTING A WHEEL- Wheels and/or moving parts.

ALL FOUR LOOKED ALIKE- Same set of wheels or engines.

THE RIMS WERE FULL OF EYES ALL AROUND- Some type of fastener, or even lug nuts. Possibly even lights.

SOUND OF THEIR WINGS LIKE THE ROAR OF RUSHING WATER- The roar of an engine or propulsion system.


All the previously mentioned key words or phrases came straight out of the book of Ezekiel. As I have reiterated many times, I try to take things as they are. As a medium, I understand that there is so much more out there if we are just willing to open our minds. I believe times change in our world. I believe that we are in a stage of spiritual awakening on this planet. I am attempting to interpret the Bible using the art of simplicity.

In the book of Zechariah, again there is a description of flying chariots.

Zechariah 6:1-5:"I looked up again-and there before me were four chariots coming out from between two mountains-mountains of bronze! The first chariot had red horses, the second black, the third white, and the fourth dappled-all of them powerful. I asked the angel who was speaking to me, 'What are these, my lord?' The angel answered me, 'These are the four spirits of heaven, going out from standing in the presence of the Lord of the whole world.'"

Here the prophet Zechariah explains what he sees as flying chariots come through a mountain pass. I believe he is again, as so many other prophets did, describing four spacecraft of some type. I also believe that Zechariah is being told, by an alien being, that the four spacecraft are the four spirits of heaven. So many times in the Old Testament, an angel of the Lord, Spirit, the Lord, or God himself is said to speak with prophets. It is my speculation that these stories can sometimes be people in the presence of spacecraft and alien beings.

In the book of Jonah, God is said to provide Jonah with a giant fish to live in for three days. He does this after Jonah falls out of a boat into the water.

Jonah 1:17:"But the LORD provided a great fish to swallow Jonah, and Jonah was inside the fish three days and three nights."

In this verse, God is said to keep Jonah safe inside a fish for three days. Let us say that you were standing next to a big body of water with a person of the Old Testament days. As you stood there, a submarine of significant size surfaced and a man named Jonah entered it. Let us also say that three days later the submarine again surfaced. The man that entered it three days earlier, now exited the submarine. You and I would fully understand what had just happened, but a person from the Old Testament days could certainly mistake the submarine as being a giant fish or whale. I believe that the story of Jonah and the whale is nothing more than the story of Jonah staying inside a submarine or submersible spacecraft for three days.

Going back to Genesis, the first book of the Old Testament, is the story of Sodom and Gomorrah. In this story, two angels come and warn Lot to take his family and leave the city because God is going to destroy it. The angels also warn him not to look back. He was told to only look and move forward.

Genesis 19:23-26:"By the time Lot reached Zoar, the sun had risen over the land. Then the LORD rained down burning sulfur on Sodom and Gomorrah- from the LORD out of the heavens. Thus he overthrew those cities and the entire plain, including all those living in the cities- and also the vegetation in the land. But Lot's wife looked back, and she became a pillar of salt."

I put this story toward the end of this chapter because I first wanted to show verses that described alien spacecraft. Having established that spacecraft are described throughout the Old Testament, now we can fully understand that there would also be weapons onboard those spacecraft. I believe these verses clearly describe a weapon. This weapon possibly had nuclear or radiation capabilities. Lot is told by the angels to leave the city and not look back.

These verses also state that God devastated the entire plain. This included the vegetation, buildings, and all the people that lived there. This most certainly sounds like an atomic or nuclear bomb was used on Sodom and Gomorrah. Lot's wife is said to look back. In doing so, she turns to a pillar of salt. I believe she stayed back from the group as they headed out of the city. She probably got too close to the field of destruction that was caused by the weapon. This, in turn, was her demise.

The last verses I want to mention in this chapter are from the book of Revelation.

Revelation 12:7-9:"And there was war in heaven. Michael and his angels fought against the dragon, and the dragon and his angels fought back. But he was not strong enough, and they lost their place in heaven. The great dragon was hurled down-that ancient serpent called the devil, or Satan, who leads the whole world astray. He was hurled to the earth, and his angels with him."

In these verses, John is telling what he sees in the future. A war in heaven, in those days, meant a war in the sky. Today, we know that most wars are fought from the sky. I believe Satan being hurled back to earth means nothing more than spacecraft or aircraft being destroyed and crashing back to the earth.

I'm sure there are many more verses in the Old Testament that could be used to make the same point that I am trying to make. I used only a portion of my notes in summarizing this. As I have pointed out in the aforementioned verses, I strongly believe that spacecraft, intelligent alien life, and advanced weaponry are talked about over and over in the Old Testament.

I believe that in the times of the Old Testament the people were describing, as best they could, what they saw and heard.

**That said, I again say that** *yes,* **I do believe in God and Jesus.** I may have a different way of getting to God and Jesus than some people, but I know that they are both real. I have stood in the presence of God. I know just how real He is. I believe the teachings of Jesus are what we should follow to find the truth, peace, and freedom that goes with being a part of God.

I think at this point you have to be wondering why if spacecraft and alien life are real, then why doesn't the government and society come out and say so? The answer to that question is kind of long. I will get into that in a lot more detail in the next chapters. As we head into the next part of this book, *Religion,* keep in mind all of the Old Testament verses; especially the ones from the book of Ezekiel. These are the verses where spacecraft are being described by the people of those days.

Also keep in mind how I explained what God is and is not. God is real. Some different belief systems may have put a slant on what a loving God He is. This may have been done to make him what they need him to be, not what he is. The chapter you have just completed will help you to better understand what I write about in the next chapter. I believe the Old Testament is, in part, a record of how alien beings and spacecraft inhabited the earth at the same time that the so called prophets were also living on earth.

In the next chapter, I will get into why I believe the government has not yet disclosed intelligent alien life.

# PART III

# RELIGION

# Chapter Six

# Churches and Disclosure

So if the government and society as a whole won't come out and disclose that there is intelligent alien life as I believe there is, then why? The answer is simple. Telling people that there is intelligent alien life out in the universe is going against everything a lot of people have been taught their entire lives. Many people simply don't want to hear it, particularly if the description involves the Bible describing these events. Like many others, I was brought up believing various pastors' interpretations of the Bible, none of which involved alien life forms. So, I am not condemning these people at all. **I am *one of* these people.**

If the government were to come out and say that there is intelligent alien life and prove it with physical evidence, such as crash evidence or artifacts, there would be a period of adjustment. The effects would be far reaching. But people would adjust and figure out that it doesn't matter. God is real regardless of alien life.

Many people's brains and lives are programmed with a belief system and they might feel lost without this GPS-like system that helps them navigate through the world. The government may be afraid of the possible fallout from disclosure, believing the human race is not ready for this change in our culture. I disagree with that assumption. I want people to understand *why* disclosure need not change their beliefs or their belief system. While there may be a change in perspective for some, their belief in God would stay about the same. This is exactly why I have written this book: to help people (who are just like me) understand that it doesn't matter how you get there, the end result is still the same.

It is my opinion that disclosure is coming and coming soon. It is part of the next step in the people on earth maturing and growing spiritually, part of the spiritual awakening I have already mentioned.

What if we found out that Jesus was conceived by his mother, Mary, through an alien father who was an alien king or ruler? My answer is simple; "Who cares." I have already stated that it doesn't matter. Jesus is still a being of higher vibration and divinity. **Jesus is still real and so is God.** As stated previously, it is likely that the biggest problem the government and society have with disclosure is they are worried about the fallout.

First, I will touch on the fallout that disclosure would have on businesses. Think about all the online retail sales of merchandise related to the Bible. Things such as Jesus bracelets, crucifixes, crosses, Bibles, books about religion, jewelry, t-shirts, and any other religious item. Or even specialty shops that sell the same merchandise. Right after the first disclosure, perhaps these businesses would take a hit. But after processing the idea that this does not need to change one's faith in God or Jesus, business would likely pick back up.

This sort of disclosure could actually cause some people to become closer to their belief system, or become more spiritual. A newfound closeness like this could be caused by uncertainty or fear. This could have the effect of some spending more money on religious items as they fully understand the implications of this knowledge. Personally, I could care less. Because I know that Jesus and God are both real, throwing some alien beings into the mix changes nothing. **My faith in God would not be affected at all**, and my faith in the government might actually improve for finally telling what I believe to be the truth.

Next, let us discuss churches. Here is where the going really gets tough. Churches are a way of life. Let me repeat that; **CHURCHES ARE A WAY OF LIFE.** They are very deeply embedded into our society. They are a part of our economy, providing jobs and security to millions of individuals. Churches own real estate everywhere and have money in the banking systems. This is a very important topic when it comes to disclosure.

The government understands how far reaching and deeply embedded into our lives churches are. They may be afraid of the financial fallout that disclosure might cause churches. Again, any such fallout would be short lived. People would adjust and accept this new information once they realized that their belief in God would remain unchanged. They could continue to worship and believe just as they always have. The only change disclosure may have on churches would be a slightly different perspective.

WHY this is such a HUGE issue? Within a three and one-half mile radius of my home, there are fifteen churches. So in less than ten minutes, I can be at any one of these fifteen churches. Not only that, but I have the choice of Christian, Baptist, Methodist, Catholic, Apostolic, Lutheran, Jehovah's Witness, Church of Christ, and Presbyterian. This is an illustration of how deeply embedded churches and religion are into our society, and likely a big reason the government hasn't disclosed alien life. This exemplifies how relevant churches are in our society.

So, numerous people believe in God. We might have a different way of getting there and that is fine. As I have stated, I am blessed to have stood in the presence of God and I know that how you get to God matters not. So what if your neighbor is Catholic and you are Baptist. You might not agree on some religious beliefs or have a different way of interpreting the Bible. Does it really matter? I say NO, it does not matter.

Let's face it, people feel good about themselves when they go to church. I know that I feel good about myself when I am leaving a church after service. I feel like I have done something good that kind of gives me a feeling of a cleansing (that I probably needed). I feel like I have done the right thing spiritually when I go to church. Like I said, it is embedded into our brains, myself included. Let us say that it was disclosed with physical evidence that there is intelligent alien life in the universe. I say *who cares?* I say to the church going people, *keep going to church*. **God and Jesus are real so keep worshipping them.**

Let us take a look at a few ways the people within church congregations do good work. God and Jesus should be the central focus, but within that focus so many helpful and altruistic gifts are shared, such as food pantries, clothing donations, Christmas and Thanksgiving baskets, repair work for those in need, and the myriad other programs churches provide. These people are doing the work of God which I consider the *work of God* to be good deeds done for other people. Stop and think about how society would change without these programs. We need churches. **They are so valuable to our society, with or without disclosure.**

As I have stated over and over, in the Old Testament, the Bible speaks more about pleasing and fearing God than it does about doing good things. In the New Testament however, Jesus speaks of helping and loving your neighbor. He also speaks of finding the truth and the freedom that the truth will bring you. Jesus teaches us to help each other. In the book of Matthew, Jesus speaks of giving to the needy.

Matthew 6:2:"*So when you give to the needy, do not announce it with trumpets, as the hypocrites do in the synagogues and on the streets, to be honored by men. I tell you the truth, they have received their reward in full.*"

In this verse, Jesus says not to brag about helping people, because your reward is in the afterlife. There are so many programs in the churches geared toward helping people in need, thereby following Jesus' teachings.

My point in this chapter is how deeply churches are embedded into our society and how far spread the churches' branches reach. Churches do so much wonderful work for society as a whole. Churches really are *temples of God and they need not change* after disclosure.

I cannot say it enough, God and Jesus are real, so even after disclosure, keep on doing the good will of God and following the teachings of Jesus. Continue to sing your songs of praise and celebrate Christmas. Keep going to church and doing all of the wonderful work that a church does. It shouldn't matter who Jesus is the son of. He is a being of high divinity who teaches us how to find our peace in God. **That peace, my friends, is in your heart.**

# CHAPTER SEVEN

# RELIGION

Up to now in this book, I have given you my thoughts. I have explained what God is and is not. I have talked about who Jesus is and why we shouldn't over think things. I have even said that spacecraft are being described in the Old Testament. I have mentioned how important churches are in our society. Now we will move forward and talk about religion.

In the last chapter, I discussed the deep embedment of churches in our society. I did this so you can fully understand my explanation of religion. You need to understand chapter six, for chapter seven to make sense. In this chapter, I want to show how some religious beliefs have been passed down for generations. I am a part of this culture as well. This deep embedding of religion goes right along with the deep embedment of churches in our society.

If the government or anyone else tells people something that is different from the beliefs that were passed down to them, then naturally there could be some concerns raised. I say to these people, go ahead and keep believing as you always have. Remember, it is okay to have different paths to the same destination. What does it matter if I say *two plus two equals four,* and someone else says *three plus one equals four?* The end result is the same.

I started my spiritual journey over fifteen years ago. I have read and researched, exhaustingly, to find *the truth* that

Jesus speaks about. I have searched in earnest to find out what the Bible says about all the topics in this book, spending countless hours and years doing so. When I got to the subject of religion, the more that I researched, the more I realized what Jesus teaches truly is the path to finding your peace with God and the eternal light. I know this because I have been where he is guiding us to be.

Often someone reads a verse from the Bible and accepts the definition of that verse given them by their leader, teacher, or pastor, and may not try to think about it beyond what they are told. This is fine. It is also fine to think about and interpret Bible verses on our own. Similarly, *it says so in the Bible* is a statement you often hear, and many making these statements don't know where in the Bible the things they are quoting were written. The point is that some people might not be proclaiming what their hearts are telling them. Rather, they are proclaiming what their brains have been programmed and taught throughout their lives. I have heard people say that the Bible is the word of God. Remember, the Bible was written by man, not God.

So, interpreting for myself, based upon careful research, is exactly what I am doing in this book. I do not mean to criticize others' interpretations of the Bible. But, I have had the privilege and life changing experience to have stood with God on a personal basis. **I can tell you that *the only word of* God is LOVE.** As a person who has read the Bible, I can only guarantee you one thing; it can be interpreted in so many different ways. You could argue all day long about your differences of opinion on one verse, let alone the entire Bible. So let us not argue, let us exchange ideas.

An example of inaccurate interpretations within the Bible includes statements about mediumship and other paranormal events being the work of the devil. This is just plain and simply misguided, and not what I have found to be true reading and studying the Bible.

A church that I have attended on occasion throughout my life says, *at this church we go by what the Bible says.* Correction, they go by what they *interpret* the Bible to say. Again, this is exactly what I am doing. I am giving my interpretation of the Bible. My interpretation doesn't mean that I am right and someone else is wrong.

If you glean nothing else from this book, please remember statements like *you better be good and follow the straight and narrow, or God will throw his wrath upon you,* are not true. God will not throw his wrath upon you. God is pure love and light, nothing else. **I have stood in his presence and been engulfed in this profound love.** I am suggesting you let your heart and soul guide you, along with the teachings of Jesus.

Some religious systems follow Biblical interpretations that go back for centuries. Whatever doesn't fit into this original religious belief system is simply rejected, forbidden. This is where religion possibly goes wrong, or too far, and following your heart and your own Biblical interpretations makes sense. Remember, the point is to find your peace, not to judge others. I believe we should use our energy to find our own peace, not waste it on judging others.

I know that I am finding my peace. That is what this book is about, finding your peace. Whatever that may be for you. However you go about understanding or worshipping God *is okay.* Do what works for you. What I offer is an alternative way of looking at what God is. Let Jesus be your guide. He can definitely send you down the right path.

In the book of John, as I mentioned earlier in this book, Jesus talks about finding the truth.

John 8:31-32:"To the Jews who had believed him, Jesus said, *'If you hold to my teaching, you are really my disciples. Then you will know the truth, and the truth will set you free.'*"

In these two verses from the book of John, Jesus tells the people if they follow his teachings they will find their truth. He says that this truth will set them free. I believe this is Jesus saying if you follow his teachings you will find your peace with God.

There could be some who tell you to do and say as they do or you are doomed. They might tell you all about the kingdom of God and how wonderful it is, but that you had better listen to them or you will miss out on it. I think this too is okay, as it is just another example of someone trying to help you. They are free to believe as they interpret things, just as I am doing. But let me make this very clear. **We are all a part of the kingdom of God right here and right now.** So when I practice mediumship and connect to God, I realize that I am already with and a part of God now.

In the book of Luke, Jesus talks about the kingdom of God.

Luke 17:20-21:"Once, having been asked by the Pharisees when the kingdom of God would come, Jesus replied, *'The kingdom of God does not come with your careful observation, nor will people say, 'Here it is,' or 'There it is,' because the kingdom of God is within you.'*"

In this passage, Jesus confirms that God is within you. This is exactly what I have been saying throughout this book. God isn't a person or place. God is the everything. You can find him in your heart.

In the final words of this chapter, I offer my synopsis of the most compelling aspects of Religion in relation to the Bible and daily life. Some traditional belief systems have a different way of looking at and accepting God than I do, and that is okay. I am just offering what I consider to be a modern, and perhaps more logical, approach to religion.

As a summary, the Old Testament shows us a God who is vengeful, angry, jealous, murderous, and hostile. A God that must be feared and obeyed. Let me make this very clear. *You have absolutely nothing to fear from God.* This is where I had to make my own choice. I could follow the God described in the Old Testament, or I could choose to follow the God that I stood in the presence of. The God I know and follow makes you feel unimaginably loved, positive, and emanating the White Light. **I chose and choose the God of the White Light and Love!** I love being a part of this wonderful God. I love following the teachings of Jesus.

Imagine that somewhere along the line man wrote parts of the Old Testament based upon the fear of what they did not understand. The fear of God came from people misinterpreting alien beings and their spacecraft for God. Imagine all the fire, fear, and anger associated with God comes from these events. It is even possible this fear based belief system may have been enhanced to keep the faithful walking the straight and narrow, or to control the population through fear. This continues down through the generations and becomes *gospel* in a way. So now you have people telling you to believe just like they do or you are doomed, because they are part of that fear based belief of *be good or God will punish you.* Fear has always been a good motivator for mankind. I say, stop fearing and start listening to your heart.

**Religion isn't about who is right or wrong. It is about finding your peace.**

# PART IV

# THE BIBLE AND MEDIUMSHIP

# CHAPTER EIGHT

# MEDIUMSHIP

In this last section, I will get into what I believe the Bible says about people practicing mediumship, which is one of the primary reasons I decided to write this book. You may be wondering why this part is in the back, if it is one of the reasons I wrote the book. At first, I was just going to write a book about mediumship and the Bible. I found out as I put my notes and over fifteen years of research together, that everything I had been studying and practicing was a part of my explanation of the Bible and mediumship. It seemed as if it all went together. I really couldn't explain the mediumship part without the other three parts of the book preceding this fourth part. I wanted to let the reader know and learn what I had learned so they could understand my point of view on mediumship.

As a practicing medium, I have been told by some that I am doing the work of the devil. I had to know for myself what the Bible truly says about mediumship. The mediumship work I do is communicating with people on the other side, in other words whose physical bodies have died. I believe that this perception of mediumship as *evil* or in some way wrong, is a misinterpretation of the Bible, just as a lot of the misinterpretations of God are.

When I am connecting a parent to a lost child on the other side, I let that parent know that their child is all right and in a wonderful place of love. I let them know that their child is in the White Light of God. I don't consider this to be the work of the devil. There is no better calling than having a child from the other side communicate through me to their parent about something the parent has done recently in their life. That is called evidential mediumship.

Evidential mediumship is the practice of telling someone on this side something that I could in no way know, and getting that information from their loved one on the other side. This is the kind of mediumship that I practice. A medium can always tell you that Aunt Susie loves you, and she probably does, but I try to get information from the other side that I couldn't know. This validates that I am indeed in contact with the other side. I try to get things like a soul's description, how they passed, things they did while living on earth, and other validating information. But I do also get those messages of love, like Aunt Susie's, that they want passed along.

As a practicing medium, and especially from standing with God in the White Light, I can tell you that there is only one theme on the other side. That theme is love. I have stood in that theme of love with God himself. And what a wonderful feeling it is.

Part of my mediumship background includes sitting in a mediumship development circle, which meets twice a month. I have learned so much from this wonderful group of people. I truly appreciate, respect, and love, every one of them. In this group, we have so many talented people. I have read dozens of books about the subject of mediumship and psychic abilities and have learned many techniques from them as well. I have done phone readings for people in different states spread out across the United States. I do local phone readings, and text or email readings. I also do face to face readings in the privacy of our home and have my own mediumship development circle which also meets at our home.

In my mediumship work, I sit in the silence every single day. I do not miss a day. This is when I either connect to a soul on the other side for someone, connect to my guides, or just ask for guidance from God and Jesus. The very most important thing that I have done in my training to be a medium is what happened before my training. That is when I had my spiritual awakening and stood in the presence of God. **Nothing compares to that experience.** That is the only reason I am here writing this book. It was the spark that my soul needed to put me back on the right path of my spiritual journey. I have had spiritual things happen to me my entire life, starting around the age of five, but this book contains a lifetime of learning experiences, and I realize that I still have so much more to learn.

Let me start off with the criticism of mediumship by some who purport it is the work of the devil. I believe that this may be a misinterpreted way of thinking that has been passed down for generations. Like I mentioned earlier in this book, Jesus' teachings in the New Testament are an upgrade to the misinterpreted belief system that sometimes can be taught from the Old Testament. By that, I'm saying that the Bible hasn't changed, but it can be interpreted in so many different ways. I realize that some might say they are not changing and are going to stick with their Bible. That is perfectly fine. Let us stick to the Bible and what it says. But what it says is only our interpretation of it.

One fine example of what I am talking about is the story of the Virgin Mary. Back in the days of the Biblical event of her pregnancy, if a virgin got pregnant one would have to think that there was divine intervention. Today we know better. We have medical procedures that easily allow a scenario like this to happen without any problems. I am not saying Mary did not get pregnant through divine intervention. I am saying that modern technology and medicine have advanced the way we look at and interpret things. Maybe we should adjust the way that we look at and interpret parts of the Bible as well. Most of the stories in the Bible were written by people who lived in a very primitive culture compared to the culture of ours today.

I believe the Bible is a wonderful tool guiding us how to live a good life and be a person who gives back to their community, is kind, and is loving. I absolutely have no problem with the Bible. I have read it and I love it. I simply believe that the way God is described and interpreted, by some, is not what and who God is. **I also believe the way mediumship is interpreted, by some, is also just a misinterpretation.**

As I have already mentioned in this book, if I am told that I am doing evil work by being a medium, because it says so in the Bible, there is a very high chance that the sender of this message probably hasn't read the Bible. They are likely repeating what they have been taught. These people have a right to their opinion. Again, I say that it doesn't matter. I just have a different way of interpreting and getting to God than they do. I welcome different ways of thinking. *It really doesn't matter how you get to grandma's house for dinner, just make sure that you get there!*

So now let us take a look at some verses from the Bible, beginning in the book of John.

John 3:16:*"For God so loved the world that he gave his one and only Son, that whoever believes in him shall not perish but have eternal life."*

In this verse, Jesus does not say believe exactly as my particular belief system does or you will not be saved. It says *whoever* believes in him will have eternal life. I believe what Jesus is saying is that your soul's life is eternal. If you want to be in the eternal light of God, then be a part of God, and Jesus' teachings. God is the light, and Jesus' teachings will get you there.

Jesus himself says it best in the book of Matthew.

Matthew 7:1:*"Do not judge, or you too will be judged."*

Here, Jesus says not to judge others. As a person who has stood in the presence of God, I can tell you that God doesn't judge you. He loves you. You judge yourself. Judging others is something that happens so often on this side of the veil. It is just a human response of the ego, and it goes against Biblical teachings. So let us not judge each other. Let us exchange ideas and have an open mind and heart.

Every time I connect to the other side as a medium, I ask for White Light protection from God. I do this so any spirit that is not from the light is not allowed in my space. So as I connect with Spirit in the White Light and feel that love from the other side, I always remember what Jesus said in the book of John.

John 13:34:*"A new command I give you: Love one another. As I have loved you, so you must love one another."*

It appears Jesus wants us to understand that love is what it is really about in the afterlife, and He wants us to practice that here on earth. From my real life experiences of standing in the presence of God and connecting to the other side, I can tell you that Jesus is right. It is all about love on the other side. Jesus obviously understands this and is trying to get this message across to the people.

Jesus says that if we have enough faith in the abilities of our consciousness, then anything is possible. I believe Jesus is saying we can do anything, just like he does, if we are willing to open our minds and hearts. These verses go right along with mediumship.

He says this in the book of Mark.

Mark 11:22-24:*"Have faith in God,' Jesus answered. 'I tell you the truth, if anyone says to this mountain, 'Go, throw yourself into the sea,' and does not doubt in his heart but believes that what he says will happen, it will be done for him. Therefore I tell you, whatever you ask for in prayer, believe that you have received it, and it will be yours.'"*

In these verses, Jesus tells us that anything is possible through faith. Now our prayers might not be answered in exactly the way WE want, or we think we want, but they will be answered in the way of the greater good being served. These verses also back up my point, *open your mind and your heart will follow.* I believe in these verses Jesus is saying that you have to let your mind get out of the way. In doing so, your heart can guide you to that understanding of the eternal light that he talks about. These verses go along with mediumship. Some skeptics might say, *you can't talk to dead people, it's impossible.* **Well, not according to Jesus.**

Another quote of Jesus' goes right along with these verses from Mark. It is found in the book of Matthew and also applies to mediumship.

Matthew 7:7:*"Ask and it will be given to you; seek and you will find; knock and the door will be opened to you."*

In this verse, I would say, yes, I agree. Every day I knock on that door to the other side and it is opened. It is opened in the White Light of God.

Also in the book of Matthew is The Lord's Prayer. I believe these verses spoken by Jesus are telling the people to live as one, in love, on earth, as it also is in heaven. I also believe that this is Jesus saying that so many things are possible on earth just as they are in heaven if you have faith and an open mind and heart.

Matthew 6: 9-10:*"This, then, is how you should pray:*

*'Our Father in heaven, hallowed be your name, your kingdom come, your will be done on earth as it is in heaven.'"*

Simply stated, I connect to Spirit from earth just as it is done in heaven.

As a medium, I believe in reincarnation. I believe souls are eternal and the body is a learning vessel used for the soul's growth and learning. Our souls are everlasting just like the light of God. Our bodies are not.

We learn a lesson or many lessons that we need to learn on each life trip to earth. Generally we are with several souls on our journey. Your spouse may have been a close friend on a different reincarnation trip to earth. Often there are soul groups learning lessons together. This is how the soul evolves, learns, and grows.

Before we reincarnate and come back to earth for another life lesson, we decide what lesson we need to learn. There can be long periods of time between each lifetime. The soul usually decides when to come back and what needs to be learned. Sometimes a guide or being of higher light might help make this decision. A soul may decide that it needs to learn the lesson of losing someone very close, like a child. So on its next life trip, the soul may decide to be put in a situation where they lose a child. They learn that lesson and then they grow as a soul.

The soul is here on earth to learn to love and grow. As the soul evolves, it moves up in the light on the other side. People who commit murder or do other evil things also go to the other side. They are just way down the pipeline. They do not see as much light. They are in the darkness on the other side. This is what most people consider *hell*. These people do go to the other side, but they are not around people who are in the light of love. They have a lot of life lessons to learn before they can begin to move toward the light.

The souls who are in the light still have learning to do, but they are way ahead of those in the darkness. There are very advanced beings of light. They are very high up in the Light of Love and God. Everybody goes to the other side after their life on earth, but a lot of them may not see the light on the other side.

I realize this is a controversial position. Some may say that you live one life and you had better get it right the first time or you are doomed to hell for eternity. In my opinion, once again we see fear based teachings that have been passed down for generations. **God knows that we aren't perfect.** That's why we are here, to learn lessons and grow as a soul. From what I have been shown, God doesn't doom you for making mistakes, he accepts you with love.

I have learned so much from connecting to the other side. This is a part of my soul's journey and I absolutely love that soul growth. In the book of John, Jesus talks about reincarnation.

John 3:3:"In reply Jesus declared, *'I tell you the truth, no one can see the kingdom of God unless he is born again.'"*

John 3:5-8:"Jesus answered, *'I tell you the truth, no one can enter the kingdom of God unless he is born of water and the Spirit. Flesh gives birth to flesh, but the Spirit gives birth to spirit. You should not be surprised at my saying, 'You must be born again.' The wind blows wherever it pleases. You hear its sound, but you cannot tell where it comes from or where it is going. So it is with everyone born of the Spirit.'"*

In these verses, while Jesus speaks of baptism as being a gesture of giving your life to God and Jesus, I believe he is also talking about reincarnation. He talks not only about being born again, but also of Spirit giving birth to Spirit. **This is the soul working its way toward the eternal light**, as I explained in previous paragraphs.

If someone is said to be doing bad deeds because they communicate with spirits on the other side, then I should point out that Jesus is the best spirit communicator of all time. It seems that some of the fear based teachings of the Bible should be looked at again with the eyes and knowledge of today. Always remember that belief systems are not made by God.

God does not belong to any particular church, religion, or system. **He IS the system.**

If you want to find your peace and grow spiritually, I suggest that you first open your mind and then your heart will follow. Sit in the silence and connect within the White Light of God. It is a lot of work and dedication, but it is well worth it. I know from experience that when I connect a grieving mother with her child on the other side, that I am doing the work God wants me to do, and Jesus tells us to do.

This chapter demonstrates how mediumship relates to the Bible. The next chapter will point out verses about using mediumship.

# Chapter Nine

# VERSES IN THE BIBLE ABOUT MEDIUMSHIP

In the last chapter, I discussed how some people might perceive mediums. In this chapter, I want to discuss what I believe the Bible says about mediums and mediumship.

First, I want to mention that the Old Testament is full of prophets and prophecy. Some prophets talked to spirits regularly. As I have stated previously in this book, I believe a lot of the Old Testament may be misinterpreted when it comes to God and mediumship. The following verse from the Old Testament speaks about mediumship. It is from the book of Joel.

Joel 2:28:"And afterward, I will pour out my Spirit on all people. Your sons and daughters will prophesy, your old men will dream dreams, your young men will see visions."

In this verse, God is telling Joel that people will prophesy, dream dreams, and see visions. He also says that he will pour his Spirit out on all people, implying that through his Spirit, people will see visions and dream dreams. This is just what I do as a medium. Through God's pouring out of his Spirit, I experience this spirit connection and visions from Spirit, on a daily basis.

Next, let us move to the New Testament, beginning with the book of John.

John 4:24:"*God is spirit, and his worshipers must worship in spirit and in truth.*"

In this verse, Jesus speaks and makes a point that God's worshipers must worship in Spirit and in truth. I believe Jesus' statement is in reference to the Holy Spirit and the eternal peace. The Holy Spirit is a part of God. To get to that eternal peace that Jesus talks about, you have to get there through Spirit. As a medium, I do that on a daily basis. I absolutely understand Jesus' message here.

Also in the book of John, is a story about Jesus after he tries to get the lost people (blind) to follow him.

John 10:19-21:"*At these words the Jews were again divided. Many of them said, 'He is demon-possessed and raving mad. Why listen to him?' But others said, 'These are not the sayings of a man possessed by a demon. Can a demon open the eyes of the blind?'*"

Here, the Jews were divided regarding whether or not to follow Jesus. Some of them thought that Jesus was divine because of the miracles he performed and they saw the good from the things Jesus did. However, they were not sure they should follow a man who spoke with Spirit and performed miraculous deeds. This really hits home for me. In my eyes, there is no better calling than connecting people to the other side and their loved ones. I work in the White Light of God, and I firmly believe these Jewish people would have approved of my work.

Again in the book of John, Jesus speaks about his abilities.

John 14:12:*"I tell you the truth, anyone who has faith in me will do what I have been doing. He will do even greater things than these, because I am going to the Father."*

In this verse, **Jesus tells us that we can do what he does**, that his spiritual gifts are also available to us. It is up to us to embrace and learn how to use them. I choose to follow Jesus in my journey, and as a medium I embrace these gifts. I do all of my mediumship work in the White Light of God and follow the teachings of Jesus as he instructs us to do.

Also in the book of John, Jesus speaks about the Spirit and all of us being as one.

John 14:15-20:*"If you love me, you will obey what I command. And I will ask the Father, and he will give you another Counselor to be with you forever- the Spirit of truth. The world cannot accept him, because it neither sees him nor knows him. But you know him, for he lives with you and will be in you. I will not leave you as orphans; I will come to you. Before long, the world will not see me anymore, but you will see me. Because I live, you also will live. On that day you will realize that I am in my Father, and you are in me, and I am in you."*

Here Jesus says exactly what I have been saying throughout this book, except naturally he says it more eloquently. Go figure (Ha Ha). Jesus tells us that the Spirit of truth, which can't be seen, will be with us always, and that this Spirit lives inside us and we are all part of one Spirit.

What Jesus describes here is precisely what I felt while standing with God. **I understood telepathically (***on that day***) that I am a part of God, because God is the essence of everything and I am a part of him.** Therefore, He is also a part of you! Also when Jesus says that, *because I live, you also will live,* I believe he is saying that his teachings are the way to the eternal love and light of God.

**Wow! These verses are a Holy Grail for anyone who has stood with God.**

Furthermore, the Spirit of Truth that Jesus says nobody can see, but which lives within us, is our soul on its journey. This journey's goal is to find that peace (truth) that Jesus talks about; the one consciousness and oneness of God and Love.

I use my soul to connect to the other side daily, often multiple times a day. I do so as I am on my journey of finding that truth. I use my mediumship to be a part of the oneness that Jesus speaks about. I also believe that when Jesus says the father will give you another counselor to be with you forever, he is referring to our Spirit Guides. Some of our Spirit Guides are with us from past lives, to the womb, and all the way to the afterlife. Everyone has Spirit Guides and Guardian Angels. **So it seems highly logical that Jesus would be quoted as talking about Spirit Guides.**

In John 16, Jesus speaks about the world fearing or hating him and his disciples because they don't know or understand them.

John 16:1-3:*"All this I have told you so that you will not go astray. They will put you out of the synagogue; in fact, a time is coming when anyone who kills you will think he is offering a service to God. They will do such things because they have not known the Father or me."*

This passage demonstrates how often people are afraid of what they do not understand, including Jesus's foretelling of events and performing miracles. Much of what Jesus did was similar to the healing mediums do today, which is similarly misunderstood.

Lastly in the book of John, Jesus speaks about Spirit being real.

John 16:13-14:*"But when he, the Spirit of truth, comes, he will guide you into all truth. He will not speak on his own; he will speak only what he hears, and he will tell you what is yet to come. He will bring glory to me by taking from what is mine and making it known to you."*

Here, Jesus speaks of Spirit guiding us into all truth, into the God-ness by giving us messages. As a medium, I receive messages from Spirit every day. I think these verses are a good example of mediumship being the work of Jesus' teachings, not the work of evil.

In the book of Acts, written by Luke, Luke speaks of the people resisting the Holy Spirit.

Acts 7:51-53:*"You stiff-necked people, with uncircumcised hearts and ears! You are just like your fathers: You always resist the Holy Spirit! Was there ever a prophet your fathers did not persecute? They even killed those who predicted the coming of the Righteous One. And now you have betrayed* and murdered him-you who have received the law that was put into effect through angels but have not obeyed it."

Luke speaks about how the traditional religious people of that time act just like their forefathers did regarding messages received from Spirit, through prophets. This is exactly the point I have been making throughout this book. Some people from that time period and of this time period, are not willing to open their minds to Spirit and Jesus' teachings and in doing so are resisting the Holy Spirit. This Holy Spirit is the same Spirit that connects all of us as one in the oneness of all that is….God.

**These verses are so telling, knowing what I have learned from the other side.** They are priceless. So I say; *Give your mind and heart a chance.* The reward is priceless.

Moving on to the book of Romans, we have Paul speaking as he introduces himself to the church at Rome.

Romans 11:29:"for God's gifts and his call are irrevocable."

**I believe Paul is telling the people that God's gifts, including mediumship, are to be used.** In other words, if God gives you a gift such as ministry, teaching, mediumship, singing, healing, athleticism, music, or any other gift, then use it! Use it in the White Light of God and for the goodness of all.

These next verses again tell us to use our God given gifts.

Romans 12:6-8:"We have different gifts, according to the grace given us. If a man's gift is prophesying, let him use it in proportion to his faith. If it is serving, let him serve; if it is teaching, let him teach; if it is encouraging, let him encourage; if it is contributing to the needs of others, let him give generously; if it is leadership, let him govern diligently; if it is showing mercy, let him do it cheerfully."

So again the Bible says to use your gift, such as mediumship, to contribute to the betterment and oneness of all involved, *the God-ness*.

Next, we go to the book of 1 Corinthians. In this book, Paul speaks about having spiritual gifts.

1 Corinthians 1:5-7:"For in him you have been enriched in every way-in all your speaking and in all your knowledge-because our testimony about Christ was confirmed in you. Therefore you do not lack any spiritual gift as you eagerly wait for our Lord Jesus Christ to be revealed."

As a practicing medium, and feeling somewhat conflicted about this, I set out to find what the Bible says about my gift. The more I looked, the more I found out that my gift of mediumship is absolutely a gift from God. **Not because of what I think, but because of what I believe the Bible and Jesus say.**

Also in the book of 1 Corinthians, Paul talks about things being revealed through Spirit.

1 Corinthians 2:8-10:"None of the rulers of this age understood it, for if they had, they would not have crucified the Lord of glory. However, as it is written: 'No eye has seen, no ear has heard, no mind has conceived what God has prepared for

those who love him'-but God has revealed it to us by his Spirit. The Spirit searches all things, even the deep things of God."

These verses are just flat out awesome! Paul states that people don't understand Spirit. He says that no one knows what it is like on the other side. I believe Jesus and Spirit hoped that by 2019, people would be a lot more spiritual and understand connecting with Spirit to a better degree. **Only fortunate people like myself know what it is like on the other side.** He also says that it is revealed to us by Spirit, which is how I connect everyday.

Paul again talks about spiritual gifts in 1 Corinthians.

1 Corinthians 12:1-11:"Now about spiritual gifts, brothers, I do not want you to be ignorant. You know that when you were pagans, somehow or other you were influenced and led astray to mute idols. Therefore I tell you that no one who is speaking by the Spirit of God says, 'Jesus be cursed,' and no one can say, 'Jesus is Lord,' except by the Holy Spirit. There are different kinds of gifts, but the same Spirit. There are different kinds of service, but the same Lord. There are different kinds of working, but the same God works all of them in all men. Now to each one the manifestation of the Spirit is given for the common good. To one there is given through the Spirit the message of wisdom, to another the message of knowledge by means of the same Spirit, to another faith by the same Spirit, to another gifts of healing by that one Spirit, to another miraculous powers, to another prophecy, to another distinguishing between spirits, to another speaking in different kinds of tongues, and to still another the interpretation of tongues. All these are the work of one and the same Spirit, and he gives them to each one, just as he determines."

Over and over in the New Testament, Jesus and other holy men tell us to accept our gifts from the Holy Spirit and to use these gifts. They say these gifts are given to us from the Holy Spirit and are meant to be used. The gift of mediumship, if used for the good, is clearly a God given gift that is meant to be used. Paul tells us, as I have throughout this book, that we all are a part of the same Spirit.

Open your minds, as Jesus tells us to do. It is so worth it. Jesus and other holy men in the New Testament understood, as I do as a medium, that Spirit is all around us and within us. It is in our hearts. These verses tell us we are all a part of the one and only God.

In 1 Corinthians, Paul again speaks of spiritual gifts and the ability to prophesy.

1 Corinthians 14:1-7:"Follow the way of love and eagerly desire spiritual gifts, especially the gift of prophecy. For anyone who speaks in a tongue does not speak to men but to God. Indeed, no one understands him; he utters mysteries with his spirit. But everyone who prophesies speaks to men for their strengthening, encouragement and comfort. He who speaks in a tongue edifies himself, but he who prophesies edifies the church. I would like every one of you to speak in tongues, but I would rather have you prophesy. He who prophesies is greater than one who speaks in tongues, unless he interprets, so that the church may be edified. Now, brothers, if I come to you and speak in tongues, what good will I be to you, unless I bring you some revelation or knowledge or prophecy or word of instruction? Even in the case of lifeless things that make sounds, such as the flute or harp, how will anyone know what tune is being played unless there is a distinction in the notes?"

Here again, Paul tells us to accept our gifts from God. He tells us to desire Spiritual gifts, especially the gift of prophecy. He tells us that the Holy Spirit wants us to prophesy. In sum, **God wants us to desire Spiritual gifts and the gift of prophecy and to use these gifts.**

As I stated earlier, one of the reasons I wrote this book was because of some of the negative talk associated with mediumship. The more that I research and reread the Bible, the more I find the Bible, Jesus, and God absolutely want me to use my mediumship skills. I am doing God's work in my mediumship. **The Bible tells me so.**

Lastly in the book of 1 Corinthians, Paul again tells us to use our spiritual gifts.

1 Corinthians 14:36-40:"Did the word of God originate with you? Or are you the only people it has reached? If anybody thinks he is a prophet or spiritually gifted, let him acknowledge that what I am writing to you is the Lord's command. If he ignores this, he himself will be ignored. Therefore, my brothers, be eager to prophesy, and do not forbid speaking in tongues. But everything should be done in a fitting and orderly way."

Over and over, Paul speaks about using the gift of prophecy, which I believe includes mediumship. In these verses, Paul says to be eager to use our Spiritual gifts, as long as we use them in a way that is for the good of all. He tells the people in these verses not to forbid such things.

Next, in the book of Ephesians, Paul again writes about prophecy. Paul writes this book while in prison. In these verses Paul tells the people to have unity in the body of Christ.

Ephesians 4:1-13:"As a prisoner for the Lord, then, I urge you to live a life worthy of the calling you have received. Be completely humble and gentle; be patient, bearing with one another in love. Make every effort to keep the unity of the Spirit through the bond of peace. There is one body and one Spirit-just as you were called to one hope when you were called- one Lord, one faith, one baptism; one God and Father of all, who is over all and through all and in all. But to each one of us grace has been given as Christ apportioned it. This is why it says: 'When he ascended on high, he led captives in his train and gave gifts to men.' (What does 'he ascended' mean except that he also descended to the lower, earthly regions? He who descended is the very one who ascended higher than all the heavens, in order to fill the whole universe.) It was he who gave some to be apostles, some to be prophets, some to be evangelists, and some to be pastors and teachers, to prepare God's people for works of service, so that the body of Christ may be built up until we all reach unity in the faith and in the knowledge of the Son of God and become mature, attaining to the whole measure of the fullness of Christ."

Wow! These verses from the book of Ephesians say so much. Paul writes that there is one body, one Spirit, one Lord, one faith, one baptism, one God and Father of all. He is over all and through all and in all. Everything is a part of the *oneness*. **That *oneness* is God.** He is the everything.

When Paul speaks of Jesus descending to the lower earthly regions, I as a medium understand what he is talking about. People in the afterlife have a higher vibration than we do on earth, which is partly why most people don't communicate with those who have passed. They don't know how to pick up on the higher vibrations of those on the other side. People on the other side lower their vibration just enough so that if we can raise our energy and vibration, we can meet them in the middle. That is how mediumship works. It is nothing more than learning to pick up on the vibration of those on the other side. We have to get our vibrations as close to theirs as we can, thus opening a communication channel. This is what I have been trying to explain, but the Bible makes so much sense out of it. Heaven is all around us all the time. We just have to learn to be aware and be a part of it all the time, or as often as possible.

Also in these verses, when Paul writes about Jesus ascending higher than the heavens, I believe he is talking about the very high divine energy that Jesus has. On the other side, Jesus is at the top of the pipeline in the White Light of God. His vibration is very high.

Next, let me touch briefly on the book of 1 Thessalonians.

1 Thessalonians 5:19-22: "Do not put out the Spirit's fire; do not treat prophecies with contempt. Test everything. Hold on to the good. Avoid every kind of evil."

Here, Paul says to test the Spirits and avoid the evil ones. **So we have THE BIBLE telling us to test the spirits and to avoid the evil ones, meaning that Spirits are a given, and communicating with them is important, and not *wrong*.** I do this every day when I ask for and use the White Light protection of God.

Another verse regarding *testing the Spirits* is in the book of 1 Timothy. Paul writes to Timothy, who is a young pastor at the time.

1 Timothy 4:1-5:"The Spirit clearly says that in later times some will abandon the faith and follow deceiving spirits and things taught by demons. Such teachings come through hypocritical liars, whose consciences have been seared as with a hot iron. They forbid people to marry and order them to abstain from certain foods, which God created to be received with thanksgiving by those who believe and who know the truth. For everything God created is good, and nothing is to be rejected if it is received with thanksgiving, because it is consecrated by the word of God and prayer."

Here, Paul tells Timothy that some people of the faith will follow deceiving spirits and demons. **I believe this is where some people might get their beliefs of mediums speaking with the devil.** I do not believe in the devil or Satan, but I do believe there are bad spirits. These Spirits are way down the pipeline in the White Light of God. This is why I always protect myself with God's White Light. Paul says that nothing is to be rejected if it is received by the word of God and prayer. This is exactly what I do as a medium. I start each session with a short word of prayer and White Light protection from God.

Staying in the book of 1 Timothy, Paul tells young Timothy to use his gifts wholly.

1 Timothy 4:14-16:"Do not neglect your gift, which was given you through a prophetic message when the body of elders laid their hands on you. Be diligent in these matters; give yourself wholly to them, so that everyone may see your progress. Watch your life and doctrine closely. Persevere in them, because if you do, you will save both yourself and your hearers."

Once again, a holy man, Paul, tells people to use their gifts wholly. He states that people can benefit by hearing messages from those who use their gifts. Think about a mother who comes to me to hear from her child that has died. **Helping a grieving mother understand that her child is still alive and well on the other side is a wonderful way to use my God given gift of mediumship.** I am helping to heal a grieving mother's heart.

In the book of 2 Timothy, Paul again emphasizes the importance of using one's gifts.

2 Timothy 1:6:"For this reason I remind you to fan into flame the gift of God, which is in you through the laying on of my hands."

In the book of James, Jesus' brother, James, writes about gifts from God.

James 1:17:"Every good and perfect gift is from above, coming down from the Father of the heavenly lights, who does not change like shifting shadows."

In this verse, **Jesus' own brother, James, states that every good gift is a gift from God.**

Lastly, in the book of 1 John. John states that God is the light, and if we walk in God's light, we are part of the one God. This is a very important point, that *God is light.* **This, of course, is the White Light that I have stood in.**

1 John 1:5-7:"This is the message we have heard from him and declare to you: God is light; in him there is no darkness at all. If we claim to have fellowship with him yet walk in the darkness, we lie and do not live by the truth. But if we walk in the light, as he is in the light, we have fellowship with one another, and the blood of Jesus, his Son, purifies us from all sin."

John continues by instructing his followers **to test the Spirits to see if they are from God.**

1 John 4:1-3:"Dear friends, do not believe every spirit, but test the spirits to see whether they are from God, because many false prophets have gone out into the world. This is how you can recognize the Spirit of God: Every spirit that acknowledges that Jesus Christ has come in the flesh is from God, but every spirit that does not acknowledge Jesus is not from God. This is the spirit of the antichrist, which you have heard is coming and even now is already in the world."

When I connect, if I am hesitant about a spirit, I ask them to leave if they are not from the White Light of God. I have never had a problem, because light always overcomes darkness. Just like in a room, if you turn on a light the darkness disappears. This is the way mediumship works. I believe this is what John is talking about when he says to test the spirits. I always make sure the spirits that I connect to, are from within the light.

In this chapter, I have pointed out many verses where the Bible says to *prophesy, see visions, use your spiritual gifts, and test the spirits.* I have quoted chapters and verses where the New Testament clearly has Jesus and other holy figures, such as

Matthew, Mark, Luke, and John, talking about communicating with Spirit. These verses state that any connection is to be done in the White Light of God. As a medium, I feel even better about what I am doing with my spiritual practice after reading and studying these verses in the Bible. Remember, I too have been brought up in that traditional religious belief system. It also is engraved into my brain, just as it is engraved into so many other people's brains. **But, I was willing to open my mind and heart and allow myself to search for the truth that Jesus talks about.**

In the next chapter, I will summarize what I believe the Bible says about each major topic discussed in this book.

# Chapter Ten

# SUMMARIZING

In the Introduction and chapter one, I shared my thoughts, explaining that while I was brought up in a traditional Christian environment, I have always been drawn to the energy of the universe and tried to keep an open mind. Over the past fifteen years, I have researched, read, studied, and used real life experiences to evaluate, explain, and answer my most pressing questions about life. I have tried to unravel how the Bible relates to these questions, using scripture as a backdrop. Most importantly though, **I wrote about my spiritual awakening and how standing in the presence of God has changed my life**. Also, please remember that I am not saying I am right and someone else is wrong. Rather, I am saying that it is okay to disagree about how we interpret the Bible, because in the end, the result is the same.

Chapter two was an attempt to explain, using scripture, what God truly is and is not. My experience of standing in His White light was that God is all-encompassing, loving, caring, and compassionate. *God is not angry; God is not jealous; God is not hostile; God is Love.* God does not care what religion you are, what your politics are, what color your skin is, how much money you have, or your sexual orientation. *It does not matter.* There is no such thing as a vengeful, angry, hostile, and murderous God. God is love. He is in your heart. You can find him there.

There is one God.

We are all a part of this one God.

God does not belong to any particular church, religion, or belief system, **He IS the system.**

In chapter three I moved on to Jesus. I believe that Jesus is a divine, high vibration, being of light. When Jesus started preaching, he used the theme *the kingdom of heaven is near.* Jesus spoke about finding the truth and peace. He tells us that we can find those things through opening our minds and hearts. This truth and peace will lead us to the eternal light. It lies in our hearts, just as he says it does. Once we find that peace, it will lead us to that everlasting and eternal light. That eternal light, my friends, is the soul warming, loving light of God.

Chapter four was about not over thinking things and trying to make everything fit into our mode of life or culture. Usually things are very simple if we are willing to look at them with an open mind. The possibilities of the universe are limitless. Through an open mind and heart the universe is timeless, just as are God and his light.

In chapter five, I tried to make sense of the God, or gods, that the Old Testament describes. Using all my research and personal experience, I arrived at the conclusion that the Old Testament, over and over again, describes not a loving God filled with Light, but rather intelligent alien beings and their spacecraft. I reached this conclusion through an open mind and knowing personally what God is not.

I acknowledged in chapter six of how deeply embedded churches are in our society, how much good these churches do, and how many people and cultures benefit from having them around. In this chapter, I also described the reasons I believe the government has not yet disclosed intelligent alien life to the public. I use the word *yet* because I believe that full disclosure about intelligent alien life is coming very soon. It may even happen before I get this book published.

As stated previously, we as a people and human race, are at the beginning of a spiritual awakening. I believe that government disclosure about intelligent alien life is a major step, in that full disclosure. Disclosure is nothing more than a growing pain for us as a species. Regarding this disclosure, remember it changes nothing with respect to God, the Bible, and most religions. Regardless of the interpretation, ultimately we still are trying to attain that oneness with God. God is the everything.

Personally, I already have intelligent alien life thrown into the mix, concerning God. My beliefs, which are listed throughout this book, will not change after disclosure. It is logical to also assume that after the church evaluates and changes some of its teachings and beliefs, and both will happen, then this book should help a lot of people better understand the changes and how they can fit seamlessly into their personal journey. This is why I feel my guides have urged me to write this book now.

Chapter seven discussed religion and how some of it can be fear based and taught to keep people on the straight and narrow. Some of us may need to understand that part of what we have been taught for generations could be an outdated, misinterpreted, fear based, belief system.

In chapter eight, I discussed what mediums are, and what they are not. Some people might tell you that mediums are doing the work of the devil. For most mediums, and especially those who work in the White Light of God, this is simply not true.

Chapter nine explains my research regarding what the Bible actually says about mediumship. I offered myriad examples of where and how the Bible discusses mediumship. Important phrases and verses were pointed out. These verses relate to the work of a medium. In this chapter, I wanted to make it clear what the Bible really says about the gift of mediumship and whether or not to use it. Many verses in the Bible, especially in the New Testament, speak of mediumship, including but not limited to the following; Use your God given gifts; Test the spirits; Prophesy; Your sons and daughters will prophesy; Your young men will see visions; Every good gift is a gift from God; If a man's gift is prophesying then let him use it; Do not neglect your gift, and many more.

I think if a person is looking to find their peace, this book will help them do that. Some traditional religions may put up a roadblock in finding that peace. If you let your heart make your decisions, instead of your culture and teachings, then you will be surprised at what you will learn.

Very importantly, as a medium, I now understand that the teachings of Jesus are the gateway to the eternal light of God. What Jesus talks about and explains as the afterlife is something that I understand because of my experience of standing with God. I didn't realize it until I wrote this book, but I discovered along the way that my mediumship resonates very highly with what Jesus teaches in the New Testament. His descriptions of the afterlife and how to get there are very in tune with mediumship and its practices.

When disclosure about alien life happens, I believe this book and the way it answers so many questions about God, the church, religion, Jesus, mediumship, and the Bible, will help a lot of people to adjust to their new reality. I believe I clearly laid out my interpretation of what the Bible says about these topics and that it will help people like me adjust to a twenty-first century approach to God and the Bible.

# CONCLUSION

This entire book is my interpretation of the Bible after standing in God's White Light. Again, I state I am not implying that I am right and someone else is wrong. Rather, the point of this book is to show that it doesn't matter how you get there. All paths lead to the same destination. That destination is the peace found in finding God. Everyone's path is different, which is why everyone's soul journey is their own. Similarly, I explained why everyone's own personal soul journey shouldn't have to change after disclosure.

A new spiritual awakening is starting right now on this planet. I encourage everyone to be a part of it. Always remember, we may have a different way of getting there, but in the end we are on the same journey and all a part of the one and only God. Open your mind and let your heart take you home. Here you are a part of the eternal light, that Jesus says will lead you to your peace and truth, which you already hold within you. This peace is God. The eternal light. His light will warm your soul. I know this.............

**BECAUSE I HAVE BEEN THERE!**

While researching and writing this book, I learned a lot about how the Bible fits in with the spiritual awakening that I have been talking about. I believe that Jesus' teachings in the New Testament are a way to cope with the spiritual awakening that is just now starting on this planet. I also believe that this book will point out and help people cope with, and understand, that spiritual awakening. *Always remember, it is not about who is* right and who is wrong. It is about finding our peace with God. As I have stated in this book, I believe that Jesus teaches us how to find that peace. I have found my peace. I hope that this book has helped, or will help you find yours!

# Final Thoughts

**IN THE BEGINNING**, I set out to write this book to find simple answers to questions about various topics, using the Bible as a backdrop. I wanted to let my own judgement and interpretation of the Bible answer these questions, rather than what I had been taught.

I did not realize what the true purpose of this book was, until I had finished writing it. My Spirit Guides had been urging me to write this book. A few days after its completion, I realized that this book was for, and meant to help, people who had been taught a traditional belief system, just as I was. This book will help people understand that even after full disclosure, both God and Jesus are real, and Church will still be a viable and good thing.

So I say, yes, continue to attend Church and worship God and Jesus if that is what brings you joy. Continue to give your money to help those in need. Continue to be a part of one of the ministries that a church or other loving organization offers. Celebrate Christmas and other holidays.

Writing this book has taught me so very much. I also discovered that I have so much more to learn as I continue my journey of finding that eternal peace that Jesus talks about. That eternal peace is God.

Can what I believe and wrote about in this book change in the future? Absolutely! **That ability to change and maintain an open my mind is what I, and Jesus, call freedom!**

In sum, this book is all about the ability to adapt to change and having an open heart that allows this change to happen. Always remember this statement, as it comes from a person who has stood in the presence of God.

*God is not vengeful, angry, or hostile. God is forgiving and loving. God is Love. God does not belong to any belief system. God is the system, and Jesus' teachings will lead you to him.*

*Also keep in mind that it doesn't matter how you get there, but I will see you at grandma's house for dinner!*

# AMEN

# NOTES

# NOTES

# Notes